THE 12-WEEK JESUS BIBLE STUDY

the

12-WEEK
Jesus
Bible Study

Readings and Reflections for
Women to Grow Closer to Christ

SHANTÉ GROSSETT O'NEAL

callisto
publishing
an imprint of Sourcebooks

Copyright © 2022 by Callisto Publishing LLC
Cover and internal design © 2022 by Callisto Publishing LLC
Illustrations used under license from shutterstock.com
Author photo courtesy of Sandy Sappington
Interior and Cover Designer: Stephanie Mautone
Art Producer: Sue Bischofberger
Editor: Andrea Leptinsky
Production Editor: Jaime Chan
Production Manager: Riley Hoffman

Callisto and the colophon are registered trademarks of Callisto Publishing LLC.

Published by Callisto Publishing LLC C/O Sourcebooks LLC
P.O. Box 4410, Naperville, Illinois 60567-4410
(630) 961-3900
callistopublishing.com

Printed in the United States of America
VP 2

To my husband, David,
and my parents, Maxine
and Oliver.

Contents

Introduction

Hi there! I am so glad that you decided to pick up a copy of this book. I look forward to walking alongside you as you study the life and teachings of Christ for the next twelve weeks. My name is Shanté, and I'm a graduate student working on a master's degree in Biblical Studies. I grew up in the Church and spent a lot of time reading the Bible and learning about the teachings of Jesus. But even though I was familiar with it, I didn't really understand the full depth and richness of scripture until the end of my college career.

My journey into a deeper understanding of the Bible began with the Gospels. I spent many hours studying Jesus's teachings and interactions with those around him. His life is the perfect model for Christians wanting to live more fully for God.

Jesus did not come to Earth just to teach us theological truths about God. He also came to teach us how to live. He did this through his words and his actions. His words touched the lives of everyone, even (perhaps, especially) people who were considered outcasts during Jesus's time.

Although many people can benefit from Jesus's teachings, this Bible study is designed with Christian women in mind. In ancient Israelite society, women were not allowed to have direct contact with God. But because of Jesus, women can know and experience God directly. His words are timeless and can touch all our lives, no matter our background or current place in life.

Wherever you are—going to school, working at a paid or volunteer job, running a household, parenting, grandparenting, you name it—this book will speak both to the special gifts you bring to the world and the unique challenges women face. As you read and reflect, the hope is that you will see how you fit into all that God has created in a way that brings you closer to him and what he wants for your life.

As you go through this study, I pray that Jesus's words will speak to you in a new and fresh way. May his teachings transform your life, and may you grow in a deeper love for Christ. By the end of this study, I hope you will understand how to live out Jesus's teachings in your relationship with God and others. By following in Jesus's footsteps, you will have the peace that comes with knowing you are living in accordance with his word, and this will strengthen your daily interactions and relationships with not just yourself but also with family and your children, significant other, friends, and/or colleagues. I look forward to guiding you through this study!

How to Use This Book

This book is a twelve-week Bible study for women covering the life and teachings of Jesus. You can work through the book individually or with a group of women. If you choose to do this as a group, there is a group study guide at the end of this book with questions to guide the group through the readings each week.

Each week contains five days of Bible readings, commentaries, prayers, and reflection questions. You'll begin with the recommended Bible reading, then you'll come to this book to reflect on that reading, beginning with the commentary. The commentary for each day's reading explains abstract concepts, breaking them down in a digestible and relatable way, and offers thoughts for reflection. Each day ends with a short prayer and questions that will give you space to dig deeper on your own or discuss what you've read with your group.

On day 6, you'll find weekly reflections, takeaways and important lessons in the week's readings, and an activity that can help you put into practice what you learned over the past week. Don't worry if you didn't have a lot of time during the week. Feel free to use the final day of the week to catch up on readings or questions you may have missed.

You can follow any format that you'd like as you work through this study. You may choose to work through this book from start to finish, or you may want to flip to a specific weekly theme. Each day's study should take approximately fifteen to twenty minutes to complete.

All you need to get started is this book, something to write with, and the Bible. This book will refer to the New International Version (NIV) of the Bible, but feel free to use whichever translation you feel most comfortable with.

Let's begin!

Weekly Devotionals

WEEK 1
Devotion to God

Daily Readings

While Jesus was on Earth, one of his goals was to show his people what it meant to live as devoted followers of God. Many people during Jesus's day did not understand what it truly meant to have love for God. Some believed that following God meant strictly observing the law without understanding God's heart behind it. Others gave many physical and material gifts, thinking that they were the best way to express their devotion to God.

But, as you will learn this week, God does not need any of those things. Following the law is important, but doing it with the right heart is even more important. Financial gifts are helpful as well, but not at the expense of love toward God.

We see true devotion to God in the lives of Christ and many of his disciples. Many of his greatest followers were women. Specifically, in this week's readings, we will encounter Mary, the mother of Jesus; an unnamed widow; and a woman looked upon as a sinner by Jesus's disciples. Although these women are far from perfect, they love God deeply and he delights in their devotion. Their lives are great examples for us as we seek to devote more of ourselves to God daily.

Mary, God's Faithful Servant

Commentary

Even though she lived more than two thousand years ago, Mary's role in Christian history still shines bright today. She is honored and loved by many in the Christian world, but she was not always viewed this way. At one point in her life, she was just an unknown young woman with no particularly significant attributes. Then, one day, she was visited by an angel. He told her that she was going to conceive and give birth to a son named Jesus.

While seeing an angel was probably strange enough, it was even more bizarre that he told her she would have a child. After all, she was a virgin and had never had a sexual relationship with anyone before!

So, she asked the angel, "How will this happen?" He responded that she would conceive by a miracle from the Holy Spirit. Her child would be the Son of God.

Her reaction here is important. Being pregnant and unmarried was cause for great shame in Jewish society during that time. Mary was to be married to her fiancé, Joseph, but he would have the right to end the engagement, assuming that she was pregnant with another man's child—not to mention the possible complications and difficulty that would come with pregnancy during that time.

Mary had a tremendous load to bear. But instead of saying, "Let me think about it," or "I'm not too sure," Mary responded confidently that she is the Lord's servant. She was willing to do the Lord's work, even though it wouldn't be easy.

In some small way, how can you demonstrate the same kind of devotion to God that Mary did? This can be as simple as staying committed to the Father and being willing to do his work, even when it feels challenging.

Lord, please help me be wholehearted and devoted to You like Mary was. Amen.

Discussion Questions

1. Who in your life exemplifies the same kind of faithfulness as Mary? How can you follow their example?

2. How does it feel to know that God doesn't want perfection, but instead devotion and faithfulness? In what areas do you think you can show more faithfulness to God?

3. Do you feel that it's more important to be faithful than it is to be recognized by others for your devotion? Why or why not?

The Widow's Offering

Commentary

In today's reading, after making his triumphal entry into Jerusalem, Jesus began teaching the crowds in the temple. He gave them a stern warning about the teachers of the law who are wealthy, prideful, and filled with false piety. These teachers prayed loud, eloquent prayers so they could receive praise from others. Even though they appeared pious, they had self-serving goals and were said to disobey God by exploiting widows in their community.

After speaking these words, Jesus sat down across from the temple treasury and watched as each individual gave their money offerings. There were plenty of rich people, and of course, they gave substantial gifts. But then he noticed a poor widow come up and give two small copper coins. These coins were worth far less than a denarius, the standard daily wage in Jerusalem, but they were all that she had and she wanted to honor God.

Moved by this poor widow's gesture, Jesus gathered his disciples and taught them a lesson. Even though her gift was worth mere pennies, in God's eyes, it was better than all the gifts in the treasury combined.

Jesus noticed this woman because she truly loved God and wanted to give her best to him. She also trusted him deeply and believed that he would provide for her. In contrast, the teachers of the law only wanted to *appear* to love God. They were already wealthy, and the abundant gifts they gave did not really cost them anything.

God is more concerned with the condition of our hearts than he is with our gifts. Today's reading does not mean that we must have absolutely nothing to serve God. Instead, it is saying that, out of love for our God, we should give our very best in service to him, regardless of how much we have.

Father, please help me give my best in all I do. May my gifts come from my heart's devotion to You. Amen.

Discussion Questions

1. Why do you think Jesus valued the widow's small gift over the more substantial ones given to the treasury?

_____

_____

_____

2. Do you ever notice yourself holding back instead of giving your best to God? If you do hold back, why do you think you do so?

_____

_____

_____

3. How can you follow the example of the widow in this story and give your best to God this week?

_____

_____

_____

DAY 3

Jesus, Deserving of All

Commentary

In today's reading, Jesus was at the end of his ministry on Earth and nearing death. Matthew explains that Jesus was spending time relaxing in the house of Simon, a leper. Matthew doesn't tell us this, but from Luke's Gospel we know that Simon was a Pharisee, an important and influential member of Jewish society.

An unnamed woman entered Simon's home, approached Jesus, and poured expensive perfume on his head. Now, this was not any ordinary perfume. It came from pure spikenard oil, and it cost a year's worth of pay. Even today, a 5 mL bottle of spikenard oil costs up to $70. In Jesus's day, this oil was used sparingly for solemn acts of devotion.

Naturally, Jesus's disciples were outraged. Did this woman not realize the value of her perfume? If she did, why would she waste it like that? What a sinful act, it seemed.

But Jesus stopped them and praised her for the costly sacrifice she had made. She was not wealthy, and we don't know how she acquired the perfume. It could have been a gift or part of a family inheritance, or she may have saved a year's worth of her salary to pay for it.

We also don't know her original intentions for the perfume. Maybe she wanted to sell it at a high price to provide for herself or to help serve the poor. Or perhaps she planned to save it for a rainy day. Regardless of her original intentions, she recognized that Jesus was worthy of this great honor. She poured her perfume on his head, preparing him for his burial. Even though it was her most expensive possession, she knew Jesus was deserving of all of it and more.

Lord, like this unnamed woman, I don't have much to give, but I give You my devotion. Amen.

Discussion Questions

1. Do you find anything relatable about the unnamed woman?

2. Is there anything in your life that you feel is "too expensive" to give to Jesus?

3. Compare and contrast the disciples and this unnamed woman. What are some similarities and some differences between the two? What do you think the unnamed woman understood that the disciples missed?

Counting the Cost

Commentary

Have you ever started a project that you weren't able to finish? Often, we start projects without realizing how much time and resources they will take to complete. Devoting your life to Christ is an important thing to do. It is what Jesus desires of us. But we must remember that following Christ requires sacrifice. Before starting this journey, we should consider how much it will cost.

Jesus taught the crowds traveling with him that they cannot be his disciples if they do not "hate" their fathers and mothers, wives and children, brothers and sisters—and even their own lives.

Wait a minute? *Hate?* That phrase is startling. However, "hating" in this context did not mean "hate" the way we think of it today. It is simply a Semitic idiom for loving less. In other words, Jesus is saying that to be his disciple, you should love him more than anyone and anything else.

This doesn't mean you should stop loving your family and friends or love them any less than you do now. Instead, it's about allowing your overarching love for Christ to strengthen the way you love others and teach you to love them better.

Jesus went on to say that those who are not willing to "carry their cross" cannot be his disciple. The cross symbolizes burdens and hardship. Being a disciple of Christ can often involve difficult experiences and struggles in life. However, just as Christ did not carry his cross forever, we won't carry ours forever, either. In fact, in 2 Timothy 2:12, the Apostle Paul says that if we endure hardship with Christ, "we will also reign with him."

Lord, being Your disciple feels costly and difficult at times, but I know it's worth it. Amen.

Discussion Questions

1. Why do you think discipleship comes with a cost?

_____

_____

_____

2. How have you personally experienced the cost of discipleship in your own life?

_____

_____

_____

3. What are some specific ways in which your love for and devotion to Christ can strengthen your relationship with your family and friends?

_____

_____

_____

Being in God's Family

Commentary

For most of us, immediate family consists of a mother, father, and/ or caregivers and perhaps one or more children. Because we live together and spend our lives with them, they tend to know us better than anyone else. Families are often great, but they aren't perfect—in fact, they can be quite complicated.

Jesus's family was not perfect, either. In fact, his brothers didn't even believe in him. If you look at some of the verses prior to today's reading, you'll find that Jesus's family thought he was out of his mind! They came to take him away from the crowd because they believed he was teaching them nonsense.

In verse 31, Jesus's mother and brothers arrived where he was teaching and sent someone to call him. When the crowd told him that his mother and brothers were outside, he told them that the ones who do God's will are his true family. You see, when Jesus came into the world, he came to bring people from all over Earth into God's family. This is because of God's great love for the world and his desire to have a relationship with anyone who would come to him. Even though Jesus cared deeply for his human family, he was especially dedicated to his family made up of those who chose to do God's will. This is because doing God's will demonstrates our devotion to him.

Your earthly family may be wonderful. Or maybe your relationship with your family is broken or complicated. But, regardless of what has happened within your human family, as a Christian, you are a part of God's family and there is nothing that can take you out of it. Your devotion to Christ and choice to follow him does not only guarantee you eternal life; it also guarantees you a place of belonging within God's family.

Jesus, thank You for giving me a
place in Your family. Amen.

Discussion Questions

1. How can you use the concept of God's family as an example in your own family life?

_____

_____

_____

2. What does it mean for you to do God's will?

_____

_____

_____

3. Do you feel connected to God's family? Why or why not? What are some steps you'd like to take to grow closer to God's family?

_____

_____

_____

Reflect and Take Action

Weekly Reflection

- Although Mary knew the potential hardship she would face as a young, unmarried mother, she still volunteered to be God's servant and carry his son, Jesus. She is admired today because of her faithfulness, not because she was the most influential woman of her day.

- God values true and genuine devotion to him more than he desires lavish material gifts. Even if you have little, God happily accepts your gifts when they're given with your whole heart.

- Devotion to God can sometimes involve costs, but God will help you when you encounter them.

- Your devotion to Christ and your decision to follow him guarantees you a place within God's family.

Activity of the Week

Jesus teaches us about the importance of genuine devotion to God. He's not asking us for perfection; he just desires wholeheartedness. We can express wholeheartedness to God by being intentional with our daily activities. Whether you are working on assignments for school or work, meeting with friends for coffee, or taking your kids to the park, aim to put your whole heart into everything you do this week. Perhaps by the end of this week, some things that once felt mundane or inconsequential may suddenly feel exciting and brand new.

WEEK 2

Our Needs and God's Provision

Daily Readings

Jesus's life and teachings often address our needs and God's provision. Jesus gives us a framework for understanding our needs and seeing them through the light of our heavenly Father's abundance. Although God is full of abundance, there are still unmet needs in the world. We experience unmet needs, and we see others in our lives and communities experiencing the same.

What should we do when our needs or those of others go unmet? And how should we present these needs to God? How should we view our heavenly Father as we approach him with our needs?

It is God's delight to satisfy our needs. We will see, however, that sometimes the forces of evil get in the way. God triumphs over these forces, because ultimately, he is greater than they are. He gives us good gifts here on Earth, but he longs to give us the even greater gift of life in his Kingdom.

Strengthened by the Words of God

Commentary

We all have needs. We get hungry, tired, and weak. Sometimes our needs are physical; other times, they are spiritual and emotional. Matthew 4:1–4 reminds us that even the Son of God had needs. Jesus was fasting for forty days and forty nights in the wilderness—he ate no food and drank no water for more than a month! Naturally, he was weak and hungry.

The thing about having unmet needs is that it can sometimes temporarily alter our character and make us weak. For example, have you ever been "hangry"? You might have a shorter fuse when you need to eat and be more prone to impatience or unkindness toward others.

But look at how Jesus responded to the devil's temptation at the time of his greatest need. Satan questioned Jesus's identity and said, "*If* you are the Son of God, turn these stones to bread." *If* you are. He meant that if Jesus was who he said he was, he shouldn't have been struggling with need in the way he was. However, Jesus refused and made it clear that it's not just food that sustains humanity; we are also sustained by the words of God.

Sometimes, when we struggle with unmet needs, we wonder if God really loves us as much as he says he does.

Here's what we need to remember: If we take our cue from Christ, we can see that God always supplies what we truly need. Jesus was physically hungry, but he was spiritually full because he feasted on the words of God. He was able to use that power to respond to the devil.

When you struggle with needs, big or small, remember that God loves you. Just because you have unmet needs does not mean he isn't with you. Your struggle won't last forever. We are not only sustained by the "food" of this life; we are also sustained by God's Words and his presence with us.

*Lord, thank You for physical food and provision. I am
also grateful for Your spiritual provision. Amen.*

Discussion Questions

1. What are some of the current needs in your life?

   _____

   _____

   _____

2. What are the ways that God may provide for your spiritual
   needs even while you deal with unmet physical needs?

   _____

   _____

   _____

3. Why do you think it was important for Jesus to refuse the
   devil's temptation?

   _____

   _____

   _____

Ask and Trust God's Will

Commentary

Is Jesus saying that if we simply ask, we will receive? Is God really *that* good and kind? He is. Yet, we often struggle to believe that he is because we see so much evil in the world and witness many people living in poverty and hardship.

Unfortunately, evil and suffering in the world are caused by spiritual forces that do not love God or his people. However, God is actively working to reverse that evil and suffering and is filling the world with his goodness.

Sometimes we ask God for help, and we don't receive the things we ask for. Let's dwell on this for a moment. Why don't we always receive the things we ask for? Some would say that there is a correct "formula" for asking for help, and if we ask incorrectly, we won't receive an answer from God. However, sometimes we ask and don't receive for the same reason that we *do* ask and receive: because God is good.

In verses 9–11, Jesus made an analogy, saying that if our children ask for bread, we wouldn't give them a stone. If they asked for fish, we would not give them a snake. Just as we like to give good gifts to our children, God loves to give good gifts to us, his children.

But if our children ask for a poisonous snake, we wouldn't give them that. If they are hungry and ask for a stone, we would not fulfill their request. God is the same way. Sometimes we don't receive what we ask for because God knows that what we are requesting may be harmful to ourselves and others. Or maybe it's just not the best thing for right now. Ultimately, God loves us and truly wants the best for us. Keep asking, seeking, and knocking. He hears you and wants to give you good gifts.

Jesus, help me believe in God's goodness.
May I be willing to boldly ask for the things
I need and trust His will. Amen.

Discussion Questions

1. In what ways have you experienced God's generosity in your life?

_____

_____

_____

2. Have you ever asked God for anything that later turned out to
   be harmful to you or others? Can you remember a time when
   God didn't give you something that ended up being a blessing?

_____

_____

_____

3. How do you personally reconcile or rationalize God's goodness
   and the evil and suffering in the world?

_____

_____

_____

God's Cares Are Holistic

Commentary

Jesus's first miracle in John 2:1–11 involves wine and a wedding. Wine was a huge part of Jewish wedding feasts in Jesus's day. It symbolized joy, hope, and the outpouring of God's blessing.

However, at this wedding, the wine ran out long before the feast ended. This was not just a mere disappointment; it was a major problem. A host who made this kind of mistake would have been viewed in a very negative light by his or her peers. Also, wine was not easy to get. The host couldn't just run to the store and pick up more. He was in a difficult situation.

Desiring a solution, Jesus's mother looked to him and asked him to help save the day. Jesus told the wedding attendants to fill up six large jars with water. They did as he said and filled them up to the brim. Next, he instructed them to take some of the water to the master of the wedding banquet. When the master of the banquet tasted it, he was amazed—it was the best wine he'd ever had.

We see that Jesus saved the day and provided much-needed wine for a wedding host whose back was against the wall. Jesus could have refused to help in this situation and could have stated that he only came to help with spiritual needs. But while spiritual needs were important to Jesus, he also cared about the earthly joy and satisfaction of those around him.

Jesus cares about our minds, bodies, and spirits and wants our needs to be met in a holistic way. He even cares about the needs that we think are too small to bring to him. It can be as simple as running late for work and wanting to catch the train on time. He hears you when you bring those needs to him.

Lord, I am grateful that You care for all my needs, not just the spiritual ones. Amen.

Discussion Questions

1. This event was actually the first of Jesus's miracles recorded in scripture. Why do you think this was his first miracle?

_____

_____

_____

2. What are some ways that you've noticed God paying attention to your mind, body, and spirit?

_____

_____

_____

3. Do you have trouble bringing "small" needs to God? Why or why not?

_____

_____

_____

DAY 4

God's Abundance: Loaves and Fishes

Commentary

As a teacher, Jesus often had crowds of people following him to hear his words. On this day, a pretty large crowd was heading toward Jesus, and he recognized that they would soon grow hungry.

Jesus asked Philip, one of his disciples: How would they be able to buy bread for the crowd to eat? Philip exclaims that it would take more than half a year's wages to buy enough bread for everyone to eat. Clearly, Philip saw an impossible situation. He saw needs to be met and not enough resources available to meet them all.

Andrew, another disciple, pointed out that a boy in the crowd had some loaves of bread and some fish. Still, they wondered, how would this small amount of food serve the entire crowd? Both disciples were at a dead end; they simply did not know how the crowd would be fed.

However, Jesus told them to have the people sit down, and so they did. Jesus took the loaves of bread and the fish from the young boy, gave thanks, and distributed them to the crowd.

Clearly, the miracle is that the young boy only had five loaves of bread and two fish and yet it was enough to feed a crowd of thousands of people.

Through this, Jesus teaches us about God's abundance. This miracle was not just about the hungry crowd. It's also meant to show that God has more than enough and longs to give us what we need.

Lord, thank You for having more than enough to share with all of us. Help me rest easy knowing that You will supply all my needs. Amen.

Discussion Questions

1. Have you ever had a need so great that you didn't know how it could be filled?

_____

_____

_____

2. What do you think you would have done if you saw the hungry crowd but had no idea how they would be provided for?

_____

_____

_____

3. How have you seen God's abundance in your life?

_____

_____

_____

Be Present; God Will Provide

Commentary

Sometimes in life, we worry about our unmet needs. Sometimes this worry can be about needs in the present, but often we worry about the future. *How will I pay off my loans? Will my friendships thrive? Will my children/parents/family be okay? Will my business succeed?*

Jesus knew that, as humans, we often worry about provision. It makes sense: We want to be secure, happy, and at peace. We want to know that we'll be okay.

However, in Matthew 6, Jesus told his listeners to do something a bit counterintuitive. Instead of worrying, he advised, seek God's Kingdom. He went on to say that while we're busy seeking God's Kingdom, God is busy meeting our needs.

In verse 32, Jesus tells us that God, our heavenly Father, knows our needs. He knows that we get hungry. He knows that we are sometimes thirsty. Finally, he knows that we need shelter and clothing. But he doesn't just know what we need; he also cares deeply for us, and he can provide for us.

Finally, in verse 34, Jesus tells us to focus on the day in front of us instead of worrying about tomorrow. Each day is filled with so much we need to take care of. If you're a mom, you may agree that taking care of your kids each day requires lots of attention. Likewise, if you are a student, you may spend a lot of time each day on assignments. Instead of spending all your attention worrying about the future, be present for these everyday moments. Be present with Jesus and the people in your life, and trust that God will provide for all your needs.

Lord, I thank You for supplying all my needs.
Help me be present so I don't miss the important
things taking place in my life today. Amen.

Discussion Questions

1. In what ways do you seek God's Kingdom in your daily life?

_____

_____

_____

2. Why is it important to be present in each moment of life instead of worrying about the future?

_____

_____

_____

3. What does it mean to trust God? How does this look for you?

_____

_____

_____

Reflect and Take Action

Weekly Reflection

- Sometimes we struggle with unmet needs. This does not mean that God doesn't love us. Any struggle we may have is temporary, and God is with us always.

- God loves to give us good gifts, just as we love to give good things to those we care about. Trust God to provide for you, and don't be afraid to ask him for what you need.

- Jesus cares about our need for joy and satisfaction as much as he cares for our spiritual needs. He desires to provide for your mind, body, and spirit.

- Jesus can provide for you even when you face the most impossible situations. He is filled with abundance and has more than enough to fill your needs.

- It can seem counterintuitive to seek God's Kingdom rather than worrying about your immediate needs. However, this is exactly what he calls us to do. When we seek his Kingdom, he provides for our needs.

Activity of the Week

This week, we learned about our needs and God's provision. As long as we live on this Earth, we will always have needs. Think about small ways in which you can bless or support someone else in your life. You can donate a service or skill that you are good at or simply engage in an act of kindness toward a person who needs it. (That would be all of us!) Choose someone to show generosity to this week and see how God uses it to fill you with joy and contentment.

Dealing with Fear and Worry

Daily Readings

Every woman can relate to experiencing fear and worry at some point in her life; let's be honest, for most of us, worry is a near-constant! Thankfully, the Bible has a lot to say about this topic. It isn't God's will for us to live in fear. Living in fear keeps us from experiencing the fullness of God's presence and the joy we are meant to have on Earth. God has so much abundance for us that he doesn't want us to miss.

What should we do about fear? We can ignore it and let it linger. But if we do that, then it will be a constant presence in our lives, right under the surface. Instead, it's better to address it head-on.

Jesus's disciples experienced fear and worry as they walked into difficult life situations. Sometimes they were fearful even though Jesus was right there with them! However, Jesus was patient with them and taught them to trust God. We'll also see how Jesus himself experienced anxiety in the Garden of Gethsemane prior to his death. However, his response to such deep sorrow and anxiety is a helpful model for us as we battle fear in our lives. We can live abundantly and generally free from fear; it just takes a little practice and daily effort.

Calm in the Storm

Commentary

Many of Jesus's disciples were fishermen, used to the sea. They would have known how to navigate its raging waters and roaring winds. Clearly, the storm in Mark 4 was different. It was sudden, terrifying, and unexpected.

You've probably had experiences like these. Life is predictable and manageable, but suddenly a proverbial storm surfaces and it's like nothing you've ever seen. Perhaps a particular "storm" is coming to mind for you. Maybe there is chaos in one of your relationships. Or perhaps you or someone you care about was diagnosed with a life-altering illness. Maybe you've lost your job, and your world seems to be falling apart.

When the disciples' world seemed to be falling apart, they discovered Jesus asleep in the boat and frantically asked, "Teacher, don't you care if we drown?" After all, how could he have been sleeping while they were suffering?

Jesus got up from his nap, rebuked the wind, and told the waves to be quiet. The sea became calm again.

Then he asked his disciples an important question: "Why are you afraid? Do you still have no faith?"

It's not that it was unnatural for them to be fearful in an event like this. It's just that Jesus was with them, and he had complete authority over the sea. He wouldn't let them drown.

When we experience storms in our lives, it's natural to be afraid. But instead of being consumed by fear, Jesus wants us to trust him. You can rest knowing that Jesus is with you. When the terrifying storms in your life are raging, turn to Jesus and let him speak peace to each one.

Lord, please help me remember that You are in control and You will calm each of the storms I face.

Discussion Questions

1. Why do you think Jesus was asleep in the boat while the storm was raging?

_____

_____

_____

2. What would you have done if you were in the boat with Jesus and the disciples that day?

_____

_____

_____

3. How have you seen Jesus calm storms in your life before? What encouragement does this give you for today?

_____

_____

_____

DAY 2

Worry Like Wildflowers

Commentary

For women, worry and anxiety tend to be a big struggle. We worry about the big problems, and we worry about the small ones. We worry about the past and the future. We worry about ourselves and our loved ones. Sometimes it seems we even conjure up things to worry about!

Jesus's words in Luke 12:22–31 are so powerful. He told his disciples that they should not worry about their life, what they will eat, or what they will wear. Notice that these needs are not frivolous. It's important to know where you will live, what you will eat, and how you will be clothed. However, it's not always helpful to worry about these things. Instead of worrying, Jesus encourages us to trust God with all our needs.

Like he often does, Jesus gave an example from nature to further explain his message. He pointed to the ravens and the wildflowers. The ravens are completely free of worry. They do not sow seeds or reap a harvest. They have no barn or storehouse in which to keep their food. Yet, God feeds them each day.

Similarly, the wildflowers grow beautifully without laboring or spinning. Jesus explained that even Solomon, one of the wealthiest kings of Israel, was not clothed so wonderfully as they are.

Of course, Jesus's disciples were far more valuable than the ravens and the wildflowers in his eyes. So, if these two examples from nature received daily food and provision, God would surely provide for them, right?

What are the things *you* worry about? How much of your time do you spend worrying? Remember, just as God cares for the birds of the air and the flowers of the field, he cares for you, too. Trust him with all your needs and believe that he will provide.

Lord, help me give my worries to You so I may trust You to meet my daily needs. Amen.

Discussion Questions

1. What are some of your worries?

_____

_____

_____

2. Do you struggle to place these worries in God's hands?

_____

_____

_____

3. What does it look like for you to trust God when faced with your worries? How can you put things in God's hands more easily?

_____

_____

_____

The Answer for Troubled Hearts

Commentary

Jesus spent a lot of time comforting and encouraging his disciples before his death. They had spent so much time with him and had grown to love him deeply. Now he was telling them that he would be going away. They had no idea what life would be like without him.

What separations have you experienced in your life? Have you ever had a good friend move away? Or experienced the loss of a loved one? Any kind of separation from a loved one can bring deep pain, but the time leading up to the separation can also be incredibly anxiety-filled. You know your loved one is going away, and though it hasn't happened yet, you fear what life will be like without them.

Responding to his disciples' fear, Jesus comforted them with these words in John 14: "Do not let your hearts be troubled." He went on to explain why: He was going back to his Father to prepare a wonderful place for them. He would return and bring them to that wonderful place. The separation would be temporary, not permanent.

If you keep reading in the chapter, Jesus also promised that he would send them the Holy Spirit, who would be their comforter. Jesus was not leaving them alone.

Being separated from someone you love can be crippling. But as Jesus said to his disciples, don't let your heart be troubled. We have a wonderful hope in Christ: All believers will one day be united with him and with each other. Whether your loved one went off to college, moved across the country, or recently took their last breath on Earth, know that because of Jesus, you will see them again. Even though fear may be a natural response, choose to place your trust in God and believe that you will see them again.

Lord, bring comfort and healing as I deal with the pain of loss. May I remember that Jesus's sacrifice on the cross provides a way for me to see my loved one again. Amen.

Discussion Questions

1. What does this passage tell you about Jesus's character?

_____

_____

_____

2. How has separation from a loved one led to sadness in your heart?

_____

_____

_____

3. How can Jesus's words to his disciples comfort you?

_____

_____

_____

More Than Sparrows

Commentary

In the age of Jesus, sparrows were seen as the smallest of all creatures, and pennies were the least valuable Roman coin. Yet, as we see in today's passage, nothing can happen to either the sparrow or the penny without God taking notice. This is because God is sovereign over all of creation, and he cares for his creations. Jesus shared this with his disciples because he knew they would be afraid when he sent them out on an important preaching mission.

The disciples were not to take anything with them on the journey except for the clothes on their backs and the shoes on their feet. Many people would oppose their message. They would be judged and rejected. Their task was not easy, and it makes sense that they would have been fearful.

Despite all this, Jesus told them not to be afraid. Why? Not because there was no serious threat or danger, but because God cared for them and was powerful enough to protect them. He protected the sparrows, and even pennies were not insignificant to him. If he cared for these things, surely he would care for Jesus's disciples, too.

Jesus went on to tell them that even the hairs on their heads were numbered. Even the most patient person in the world wouldn't be able to sit and count all the hairs on their heads. And who cares how many of them they have? God. He knows how many hairs are on each and every one of our heads, because he cares for us even more than we care for ourselves. He promises to keep us safe in the face of danger, and we are worth far more than sparrows to him.

Lord, as my loved ones and I go out into the world and face challenges each day, please be with us and guard us from all danger. Amen.

Discussion Questions

1. Why do you think Jesus allowed the disciples to experience situations where they might be judged and rejected?

_____

_____

_____

2. What are some of the challenges that await you and those you care about today?

_____

_____

_____

3. How does the knowledge that God is both sovereign and caring help you through your challenges?

_____

_____

_____

Thy Will Be Done

Commentary

In today's passage, Jesus was filled with so much sorrow as he faced his death that his sweat became like drops of blood falling to the ground. In just a few hours, the weight of the sins of the entire world would be placed on his shoulders. He would die a cruel death and hang on the cross alone, separated from the love of the Father.

It wasn't so much the thought of death that caused Jesus's anxiety. It was the impending judgment that he would receive from the Father for sins he did not commit. He would drink of the cup of God's wrath, something that was only poured out on sinners.

Some argue that Jesus's emotions in the garden have nothing to do with anxiety. This is probably because they associate anxiety with sin. While it is true that God does not want us to live in a state of anxiety, it isn't a sin.

It is certainly arguable that Jesus's emotions in the garden did include anxiety. He was sorrowful and prayed earnestly because he knew what agony would await him in the future. He would face death and momentary separation from his Father.

But notice what Jesus did with this anxiety. He didn't ruminate on all the negative possibilities that the future would hold. Instead, he prayed earnestly to the Father. Although he would have to face intense suffering, he knew that his Father was good and loved him. He was able to say, "Not my will, but yours be done."

Do you ever feel anxious about situations outside your control? How you respond to this sort of anxiety is important. Whether it is anxiety over a job-related issue, your child's welfare, or test results from your doctor, turn to the Father in prayer and give your anxiety over to him.

Lord, please help me follow Jesus's example whenever I feel anxious about the future. Teach me to pray earnestly to You and believe that You are good. Amen.

Discussion Questions

1. What are some things you feel anxious about right now?

_____

_____

_____

2. What do you think it was like for Jesus to be momentarily separated from God's love?

_____

_____

_____

3. How do you demonstrate your trust in God in the face of difficult situations?

_____

_____

_____

Reflect and Take Action

Weekly Reflection

- Uncertainty in our lives can naturally lead to fear. We must remember that Jesus is with us, and he can speak peace to every one of our uncertainties.

- We don't have to worry about the future because God is in control of it. Instead of taking the burden of your needs on yourself, give that burden to Jesus.

- It is easier said than done, but we do not have to be afraid when separated from a loved one. Carry the faith that you will one day see your loved one again.

- God's love extends from the smallest creatures on Earth to the smallest details of your body. He is sovereign and loves you enough to take care of each of your needs.

- Jesus's response to his anxiety in the Garden of Gethsemane is a model for us. He gave his anxiety to the Father through prayer because he knew that his Father was good and loved him.

Activity of the Week

Fears and worries will inevitably come up for you this week. Instead of allowing them to linger or feeling shame that they're there, write about them. Be honest with yourself and with God about what you are feeling. At the end of the week, take that piece of paper and bring it before God. Look up what the Bible says about each fear. Write a related Bible passage below each fear in a different color pen. Keep the sheet of paper handy so that when those fears surface again, you can be reminded of God's truth about the situation through scripture.

WEEK 4
Remarkable Faith

Daily Readings

F aith is an important theme not only in Jesus's teachings, but in all of scripture. Think of faith as the door that allows one to enter the Kingdom of God.

This week, you'll read about a woman with a blood disorder who was bold in her faith in Jesus. You'll also encounter a Gentile woman who demonstrated remarkable faith and pleaded with Jesus to cleanse her daughter of demons. You'll discover the faith of a blind man who recognized Jesus's identity as the Messiah and a centurion who understood Jesus's power to heal. Finally, we'll explore together the difference between faith in oneself and faith in God.

As you read, remember that faith is meant to bring us closer to God. His will is not the same thing as a genie granting wishes. God works in far more mysterious and subtle ways, and besides, the goal of faith is about something bigger. The ultimate blessing we receive through faith is our salvation. While faith may produce blessings or healing here on Earth, it does not always have such a visible impact on our daily lives. Many people have strong faith and still battle with sickness, pain, and hardship. When we do receive the good things we desire, it is a reminder of the greatest blessing: that one day God will bring us into his eternal Kingdom, where all that is wrong will become right again.

DAY 1

Faith Can Heal

Commentary

In Luke 8, Jesus was on his way to the house of Jairus, a Jewish leader, to heal his sick twelve-year-old daughter who was on the verge of death. Suddenly, a woman emerged from the crowd and reached out to touch the bottom of his cloak. She had been sick with a blood disorder for twelve years and no one could heal her. As soon as she touched Jesus, her bleeding stopped.

This woman demonstrated remarkable faith in several ways. First, she courageously came out to see Jesus, even though the law forbade her from socializing with others because of her disorder. Jewish law stated that anyone with a discharge of blood was unclean and had to live outside of society until the condition was resolved. Next, she believed that Jesus could heal her. Even though she had suffered for many years and no one had been able to help, she trusted that there was something great about Jesus that could help her situation.

As an outcast, she did not have the luxury of asking Jesus for healing the way that Jairus did. She had to crawl through the crowd and desperately grab hold of his clothing. She didn't care what the crowd thought or what trouble she might get into with the Jewish authorities. Her focus was only on getting close to Jesus.

When Jesus recognized what had happened, he said to her, "Your faith has healed you." The healing came from Jesus, but the woman's faith and trust in him is what led her to receive the life that was constantly flowing from him.

You may have some things in your life that require healing: Maybe it's a common cold, chronic pain, or a battle with infertility. Reach out to Jesus and trust him with the same remarkable faith this woman demonstrated.

May I put my faith in you, Jesus,
whenever I need healing. Amen.

Discussion Questions

1. Why do you think this woman's story is placed in the middle of a larger story (the story of Jairus)? What does this teach us about Jesus and his desire to heal?

_____

_____

_____

2. What are some areas in your life that you are looking for Jesus to heal?

_____

_____

_____

3. How have you seen your faith in Jesus grow stronger as you've waited for healing? How can you grow it even more?

_____

_____

_____

A Gentile Woman's Faith

Commentary

Jewish people living in the first century believed that salvation was only for Jewish people. Technically, Jesus's primary mission was to the Jews. This is why we see him healing, performing miracles, and preaching to Jewish people early in his ministry. However, it was God's plan that the entire world would have an opportunity to be saved. Therefore, Jesus ministered to more than just Jews; he also reached out to non-Jews, or Gentiles.

In today's reading, Jesus traveled to Tyre, an area with a large Gentile population. He did not want to make his presence known, but a woman noticed him in town and pleaded with him to cast a demon out from her young daughter.

Jesus's response was puzzling. Metaphorically, he told her that the "children," or the Jewish people, deserve to receive all they need from him and the "dogs," or the Gentiles, do not. There was a lot of tension between the two groups, and this was the status quo. In fact, Jesus's conversation with this woman was already unusual—Jewish rabbis did not speak to women, especially non-Jewish women.

Surprisingly, the Gentile woman did not take offense to Jesus's words. She continued to plead with him for her daughter's sake. He noticed her persistence and immediately set her daughter free from the demon.

Jesus is nondiscriminatory in his actions. Regardless of his words, since he is divine, he already knew ahead of time that Gentiles were on God's agenda, and he loved them as much as he loved the Jewish people. Salvation was not just for the Jews; it was for everyone who would believe in Jesus. Faith is the means through which one receives healing, freedom, and salvation. It has nothing to do with class, ethnicity, or status.

Lord, I thank You that faith, not status, gives me a place within Your family. Amen.

Discussion Questions

1. Have you ever been excluded based on your status, gender, or beliefs? Have you ever excluded others? What would be a good Christian way of responding to either of these situations?

_____

_____

_____

2. Why do you think faith, not status, is the key to being a part of God's family?

_____

_____

_____

3. What steps do you take to welcome and be inclusive toward people who are different from you?

_____

_____

_____

Mustard Seed Faith

Commentary

Someone gave me a mustard seed once. I knew that mustard seeds were supposedly very small, but I hadn't seen one in person until that moment. It was so small that if I dropped it on the ground, I'd probably struggle to find it again. Yet, in Matthew 17, Jesus tells his disciples that's how much faith was needed to drive a demon out of a young boy.

The story in Matthew 17 starts with a man who approached Jesus and asked for healing for his son who was being tormented by demons. The man had previously brought his son to Jesus's disciples, but they were not able to heal him.

Notice the frustration from Jesus in verse 17: He referred to the Jewish people as "unbelieving" and "perverse." Why? He was astonished at their lack of faith. The crowds saw many of Jesus's miracles, yet they still struggled to have faith.

Of course, Jesus healed the boy and freed him from the demons. After this, the disciples asked Jesus why they couldn't drive out the demon. His reply was that they had little faith.

Remember that mustard seed? It's not that they needed a huge amount of faith; they just needed faith the size of a tiny mustard seed, and then they could do what seemed impossible. But their faith needed to be oriented toward God, not themselves.

Maybe you need restoration in your relationships, or perhaps you're praying that a loved one will come to know Christ. It can be frustrating when you're trying your best to help and nothing seems to be changing. But sometimes situations don't change just because you've been trying hard. Jesus wants you to put your faith in God. Remember that, while some miracles happen instantly, others may take more time.

Jesus, I am grateful that I do not need a ton of faith to see You doing the impossible in my life; I merely need to turn my faith toward You. Amen.

Discussion Questions

1. How do you feel about your faith today? Is it pointed more inward or more toward Christ?

_____

_____

_____

2. Why do you think some miracles aren't always instant today?

_____

_____

_____

3. What do you feel is the difference between having faith in your own abilities and having faith in God? How can you shift your faith?

_____

_____

_____

Faith in Love, Not in Sight

Commentary

Remember how yesterday we spoke about Jesus's frustration at the Jewish people's lack of faith? Well, today we get to look at a passage that shows great faith. Jesus and his disciples had just arrived at Jericho, and Bartimaeus, a blind man, was sitting on the side of the road. He understood that Jesus was passing by, and he began shouting, "Jesus, Son of David, have mercy on me!"

This is huge. It's not just that Bartimaeus recognized that Jesus could heal him. No, he recognized *who* Jesus was. The Old Testament tells us of a figure known as the Messiah, who would descend from King David and bring restoration, healing, and salvation to the Jewish people. They often referred to this figure as the Son of David.

Unlike the crowd, this man did not have physical sight, but he saw spiritually and knew that Jesus was the Messiah. Even though the crowds followed Jesus, they did not all know who he was. Eventually, the same crowd would call for his crucifixion.

Jesus asked Bartimaeus what he wanted, and he said, "I want to see." After Jesus healed him, Bartimaeus joyfully followed Jesus.

Jesus's miracles were not performed to get the attention of crowds. The miracles were simply a sign that God's Kingdom was coming, and those who followed Jesus could be a part of that Kingdom. Bartimaeus's response to healing exemplifies the way we should respond when Jesus does something great in our lives. Have you been praying for friends who can help you grow in your faith and hold you accountable? Or for a job that you love and would thrive in?

When God answers, allow this to stir up more love for God in your life. True faith is not just believing that Jesus can do something for you and letting it happen; true faith is about love and discipleship.

May I remember that the good things Jesus does for me are meant to point me to Your Kingdom. Amen.

Discussion Questions

1. How do you feel about Bartimaeus's strong spiritual connection that allowed him to feel Jesus's presence with such clarity?

_____

_____

_____

2. What are some things Jesus has done for you recently?

_____

_____

_____

3. How can you take action and respond with greater love toward Jesus when you see him working in your life?

_____

_____

_____

Just Say the Word

Commentary

A centurion was a commander in the Roman army. Such a rank in the army of the most powerful empire at the time equated to a lot of authority. The centurion had soldiers and servants who listened when he spoke and obeyed his commands. But even so, he came to Jesus and asked for his help. One of his servants was suffering from paralysis.

When he asked, Jesus offered to come to the centurion's home and heal the servant. But the centurion expressed that he did not deserve Jesus's presence in his house. In the ESV translation of the Bible, he says, "I am not worthy to have you under my roof." Technically, as a Roman commander, he would have had authority over the Jewish people, including Jesus. But he recognized that Jesus was greater than he and was no ordinary Jewish man.

Instead of asking Jesus to come to his home, he said, "Just say the word, and my servant will be healed." He had so much trust in Jesus that he knew his servant would be okay with Jesus just saying a word.

Jesus's response? He told his followers that he had never seen such great faith in Israel. This man was not even Jewish and yet demonstrated greater faith in Jesus than the Jewish people did. Because of his faith, not his status, the centurion would have a place in God's Kingdom. By just speaking the word, Jesus healed his servant instantaneously.

Faith is simple, and yet it can seem challenging. It's not about how much faith you have; it's about who your faith is oriented toward. Do you believe that Jesus has the authority to step into the hard places in your life? He can, and all he needs to do is say the word.

Jesus, please speak Your word and bring change to the challenging situations in my life. Amen.

Discussion Questions

1. How do you think Jesus would describe your faith?

_____

_____

_____

2. Do you feel that it's challenging to have faith in Jesus? Why or why not?

_____

_____

_____

3. How can you follow the Roman centurion's example of faith? How about humility?

_____

_____

_____

Reflect and Take Action

Weekly Reflection

- It doesn't matter who or what may be keeping you away from Jesus. Push through the "crowd" to get close to him. Consider how your faith in him will be able to heal you or give you freedom from the struggles you face.

- Jesus does not discriminate. The gift of God is for all who come to Jesus by faith. Class, ethnicity, or status have nothing to do with God's Kingdom.

- A mustard seed is a very small thing, yet Jesus says this is the amount of faith we need to see the impossible done in our lives. Who our faith is turned toward is more important than the amount of faith we have.

- Our response to the things Jesus does in our lives should be more than simply accepting; instead, may it multiply our faith and love for him.

- Many people recognized Jesus's authority to heal, without literal or figurative sight. We can strive to recognize his authority to bring healing into our lives.

Activity of the Week

We talked about mustard seed faith in one of this week's readings. If you can, purchase some mustard seeds. If you can't, look for the smallest stone you can find outside. Put your mustard seed or small stone in a small container and place it where you will be able to see it often, or you can even place the seed in a mini cork bottle and turn it into a pendant to wear as a necklace.

Solitude and Rest

Daily Readings

This week we will discuss the value of solitude and rest in our lives as followers of Jesus. Rest is not only an important theme in the Gospels; it's also central to all of scripture. We see that God rested from his work after creation. Although he did not need to rest, he did so to set an example for us. As humans, we often get tired and weak. We need rest to renew our strength so we can continue doing the work God calls on us to complete. This is especially true for women who care for others—we can't pour from an empty cup!

As you take time to study this week, you'll learn about Jesus's light and easy yoke and the rest he gives us for our souls. You'll also explore why it's sometimes necessary to rest even when our work is not finished. Finally, you'll contemplate the purpose of the Sabbath and the value of having quiet, intentional places in which to experience solitude and spend time in prayer with God. Ultimately, our rest here on Earth foreshadows the rest we will enjoy in heaven. As you read about Jesus's teachings, take time to consider how you can prioritize rest just as he did.

Rest for Your Soul

Commentary

In this reading, after praying to his Father, Jesus invited those who were weary and burdened to come to him. In verse 29, he hinted at the source of their burdens. He tells them to take his "yoke," his teachings about life with God and others, and learn from him. Literally, a yoke was a wooden frame that joined two oxen together and allowed them to carry heavy loads. However, figuratively, a yoke represented the Jewish law. The Jews were burdened by the leaders and their unrealistic expectations for how people should practice the law.

Jesus was saying to them: Exchange your heavy yoke for mine. Yours is too much to carry, but mine is easy and light. God never intended the law to be a burden for his people. In fact, it was a temporary measure put in place until Jesus came to Earth. When Jesus came, he taught the correct and burden-free way to fulfill the law. God's people no longer had to carry a heavy burden; they could have rest for their souls.

Have you ever been a part of a community that had so many rules that it felt like a burden? Rules are important, but sometimes humans create more rules than necessary. Often, these rules are arbitrary; many more stem from fear. For example, the Jewish leaders feared that without all their rules, God would not rescue them from the Romans. They believed that if they put an expectation of perfection on the Jewish people, God would send someone to save them.

You can rest from unrealistic expectations. Taking on excessive burdens will not make your life perfect, nor is it what God wants for you. Instead, a fulfilled life comes from taking on Jesus's yoke, listening to his teachings, and trusting him with everything as you spend your time living among and loving his wondrous creations.

*Lord, help me lay my burdens at Your feet and
take on Jesus's yoke instead of my own. Amen.*

Discussion Questions

1. Can you relate to the Jewish leaders' belief that perfect compliance with their laws would cause God to save them? Why or why not?

_____

_____

_____

2. What are some of the burdens you've had to carry in your life? How can you set them down?

_____

_____

_____

3. How would you compare Jesus's yoke with yours?

_____

_____

_____

The Gift of Rest

Commentary

Today we meet two sisters, Mary and Martha. They were close friends of Jesus, but they are often pitted against each other in Christian culture. One day, Martha invited Jesus into her home. When he arrived, she began making preparations so that he would enjoy his time in her home. Meanwhile, Mary sat at Jesus's feet, listening to his words.

Martha was upset that Mary wasn't helping her with any of the work, and so she asked Jesus to do something. Jesus's response was interesting: "Martha, Martha," he said. "You are too worried."

This is a difficult passage. Of course, the work needed to be done. If someone was not cooking, no one would eat. But at the same time, it was just as important for Mary to listen to Jesus's teachings.

Have you ever felt worried or anxious while preparing to host someone in your home? You may have frantically run around, trying to make sure the linens were clean, the table was set, and the food was ready. It's natural to want everything to go well when you have a guest. But sometimes we need to rest, even when the work is not perfectly done. Rest is a gift, not something we earn only after we have checked all the boxes on our to-do list.

Yes, there is a time to work, but there is also a time to rest. In this story, it was Mary's time to rest, and this blessing would not be taken away from her. You, too, can recognize when it is your time to rest. Be sensitive to the Holy Spirit when he encourages you to lay down some of your worldly work. Spend time with Jesus and allow him to refresh your soul.

Lord, I often struggle to rest. May I remember that it is a gift from You that I can enjoy regularly. Amen.

Discussion Questions

1. What stands out to you from Jesus's interaction with Mary and Martha?

_____

_____

_____

2. Do you feel like you relate more to Mary or Martha in this story?

_____

_____

_____

3. Have you been regularly using the gift of rest? Why or why not? How can you shift your thinking to include more rest?

_____

_____

_____

The Sabbath: Made for Humanity

Commentary

The Sabbath was a huge part of Jewish culture. Every seventh day, the Jews were commanded to rest from their work and spend time in God's presence.

In today's passage, we see Jesus's disciples working on the Sabbath. This was strictly forbidden. The Jewish leaders, or Pharisees, questioned Jesus about his disciples, asking why they were picking grain on the Sabbath. Jesus responded by alluding to the Old Testament: King David and his companions ate consecrated bread from the temple when they were hungry. Technically, only the priests were permitted to eat this bread. Jesus's disciples picked grain because they were hungry. The Pharisees' overinterpretation of the law meant that hungry people would have to starve in order to practice the law according to their standards.

Then Jesus said something profound: "The Sabbath was made for man, not man for the Sabbath."

The Sabbath was not meant to be a burden. God gave his people the Sabbath as a gift. He wanted them to enjoy the same kind of rest he enjoys. The Sabbath was a reminder for the Jewish people to work from a place of rest and contentment. Have you ever worked on a hobby or project you were particularly passionate about? In contrast, maybe you have a job that only pays the bills. Sabbath rest is like working on your passion project. There may still be work to be done, but doing that work is filled with ease and joy.

Likewise, in today's culture, we hear a lot about self-care. It's important! But sometimes the world's standards of self-care can feel like a burden that inhibits true rest. There isn't a perfect way to rest. The most important thing is being with God, spending time with friends and family, and enjoying the gifts God has given you.

Lord, thank You for the gift of the Sabbath. Help me enjoy it as a gift and not a burden to carry. Amen.

Discussion Questions

1. What does Sabbath rest look like for you?

_____

_____

_____

2. Do you find yourself falling into the trap of making rest a burden? How?

_____

_____

_____

3. How do you think the mindset of seeing the Sabbath as a gift can fill your work with ease and joy?

_____

_____

_____

DAY 4

Quiet Places

Commentary

In the beginning of Mark 6, Jesus sent his disciples out to preach, heal, and drive out demons. In verse 30, they returned, tired and hungry, and told Jesus about the wonderful things they had done. But there were crowds of people coming toward Jesus. Instead of attending to the crowd, Jesus told his disciples to come with him to a quiet place and get some rest. So, they got into a boat and sailed away to a solitary place.

In today's world, we don't often take time to rest when we are tired. In this light, Jesus's response may seem unusual. Why would he suggest going away when so many people needed them? You may think they should have addressed the needs of the crowd first. But no—they were tired and weary from all their work and needed time to refresh.

Can you relate? Perhaps you've spent all day mentoring other women, managing important projects, or attending to your children at home, but more tasks await you. May Jesus's words in verse 31 give you permission to rest, even if your work isn't completed yet.

Now notice verses 33 and 34: The crowd was so desperate for Jesus and the disciples that they ran ahead and arrived at their destination before Jesus did. Though the disciples' rest was interrupted, Jesus had compassion for the crowd and taught them. If you have children or are a caregiver, you probably know what this feels like! Follow Jesus's example and seek out rest when you need it. You can be flexible as well, recognizing and attending to urgent needs when necessary, but it's okay (even important) to take care of yourself.

Lord, help me prioritize rest in this busy, fast-paced world. Teach me to follow Jesus's example and allow myself to take time to refresh when I am tired.

Discussion Questions

1. What stands out most to you about Jesus's words and actions in this reading?

_____

_____

_____

2. Jesus and the disciples went in a boat to a quiet place. Do you see value in having a designated quiet space for rest? Why or why not?

_____

_____

_____

3. What are some things you can do to make room for rest in your busy schedule?

_____

_____

_____

Solitary Prayer

Commentary

In today's reading, we get to witness another great miracle of Jesus. He healed Simon's mother-in-law, who was sick with a fever. After this, he healed many other sick and demon-possessed people. Finally, an entire town of people gathered at the door to the home where he was staying, and he healed their diseases, too.

Instead of focusing on the miracles, look at what Jesus did afterward. In verse 35, Jesus got up early in the morning, left Simon's house, and went to a solitary place to pray. He spent time resting in his Father's presence after performing many wonderful miracles.

While it's easy to focus on Jesus's healing ministry when reading the Gospels, we should also notice how Jesus rests and communes with God in between the miracles. Even though there was always a crowd who needed Jesus, he did not neglect time with God. He regularly took time to pray and just be with his Father.

When life gets really busy, it can be a struggle to make time for God. We may think that we'll just finish all the work first and *then* spend time with God. However, we know the work is never really finished! Ironically, it is our time with God that provides the strength to complete our work. Neglecting to rest in God's presence can lead to burnout and exhaustion. Conversely, time with God revives us and reminds us that life is about so much more than our work.

Spend time with God in solitary prayer. Even a few intentionally spent minutes are enough to help strengthen us for the work that lies ahead.

*Lord, thank You for the gift of solitary prayer.
I don't often prioritize this gift, but help me do so and
strengthen me for the daily work that life brings.*

Discussion Questions

1. Do you view solitary prayer as a gift? Why or why not?

_____

_____

_____

2. Why do you think scripture values rest? What does this say about God's character?

_____

_____

_____

3. How can you make time to rest and enjoy God's presence, even with a busy schedule?

_____

_____

_____

Reflect and Take Action

Weekly Reflection

- Unrealistic rules and expectations are heavy burdens no one should have to carry. Exchange that burden for Jesus's light and easy yoke and find rest for your soul.

- Rest is not something we earn after checking off the boxes on our to-do lists. It's a gift that we can enjoy at any time.

- The Sabbath was put in place to serve humanity, not the other way around. The most important part of the Sabbath is being with God, spending time with friends and family, and enjoying God's wonderful gifts.

- Sometimes we need to take time away from our work and refresh in a quiet place so we can be recharged to continue attending to the needs of others.

Activity of the Week

This week, go to your quiet place. If you don't have a quiet place where you can go to rest and pray, take this week to find one and make it your own. It could be a spot in your home or a bench at a park in your neighborhood. Take time to rest from your work for a few minutes each day and spend time with God in your quiet place. Perhaps you can pray or read the Bible, or maybe you can just sit in silence with God. Do what you need to rest, recharge, and connect with God.

WEEK 6

Grief

Daily Readings

Grief is defined as a deep sorrow, and we often associate it with the kind of sorrow that is caused by someone's death. Grief is a painful emotion that many of us have had to wrestle with at some point in our lives. While grief can be caused by the loss of a loved one, it can also be the result of other things, such as the loss of a job, making a mistake, or even a fear of the future. Though grief is unique to each person and can be difficult to process, the Bible gives us lots of wisdom to help us do so.

This week, we will explore how Jesus and his disciples grieved various sorrows. You will also see how grief can be followed by hope and healing. Although Jesus was divine, he went through grief, just like all humans do. He felt pain at the death of his friend Lazarus and dealt with grievous sorrow when he hung on the cross, forsaken by God.

While it is a natural reaction to want to ignore our grief, we must take the time to walk through it and process it in order to come out stronger on the other side. The Christian belief is that there is healing for all forms of grief and pain; however, there is no timeline for grief caused by loss—it's unique to each person. We will also learn that lingering in sorrow and grief over past mistakes for too long can be harmful to our lives. In certain situations, moving on at the right pace is just as important for our healing journey, and in doing so, we can make amends to quell the grief.

Jesus Wept

Commentary

Lazarus was a good friend of Jesus. He was the brother of Mary and Martha, the women you were introduced to in Luke 10. Lazarus became sick and died, leaving his loved ones filled with grief and pain. Mary and Martha had called for Jesus while Lazarus was still sick. However, he stayed away for two reasons: First, going to Judea, where Lazarus was, would have been dangerous for Jesus, as the Jewish leaders there were there trying to kill him. Second, and more important, he knew that Lazarus's sickness would not end in permanent death. Jesus would perform a miracle and God would be glorified.

Before the miracle, however, Jesus expressed deep grief and sadness over Lazarus's death. In today's reading, Mary saw Jesus and remarked that if he had been there, her brother would not have died. Jesus noticed her tears and was moved with compassion. He asked to see Lazarus's body, and upon seeing him, Jesus wept over his friend.

The shortest verse in the Bible—John 11:35—is also one of the most powerful: *Jesus wept*. Yes, he was divine, but he was also a human being. He had feelings and experienced a wide range of emotions, just like we do.

Jesus eventually raised Lazarus from the dead, but not before taking time to grieve.

Have you lost a loved one or felt immense sadness over a significant loss in your life? Grief is not a fun thing to go through. It is heartbreaking and can feel like walking through a dark valley. Still, the only way out of the valley is to go through it. Although challenging, processing our pain can bring healing and the ability to live with our loss, and we can take comfort in knowing that Jesus walks with us and intimately understands our suffering.

Lord, please help me do the difficult work of walking through the valley of grief. It's not the place where I want to be, but I know that processing the pain of my loss can bring healing. Amen.

Discussion Questions

1. Why do you think the Gospel writer portrays Jesus's grief and sorrow?

_____

_____

_____

2. Have you ever experienced God's comfort through loss? What was it like?

_____

_____

_____

3. How do you suppose that making space for grief can help you heal?

_____

_____

_____

Grief Turned to Joy

Commentary

In John 16, Jesus hinted at his soon-approaching death and resurrection. He told his disciples that shortly they would no longer see him, but soon after that, they would see him again. The disciples would weep and mourn at Jesus's death while the world would rejoice. However, their grief would not last forever. It would soon turn into joy.

Jesus continued by sharing an analogy about childbirth. If you are a mother, you may have experienced the pain that can come with childbirth. However, you may also know that seeing your child for the first time can make you forget (or at least be okay with) the pain. The purpose of the pain was to lead to the joy of a newborn child, and once your child arrived, the pain was no longer important.

In verse 23, Jesus told the disciples about the coming Day of the Lord, a day of hope for believers in Christ. He told them that on that day, they would no longer ask him anything. Though this phrase is vague, he may be speaking of questions they had concerning his death and resurrection. After all, the disciples were often confused about why he needed to die and rise again. On this day, they would have full clarity about the purpose of Jesus's death. They would also pray to the Father in Jesus's name and receive the things they asked for. This and so much more would come, but only after their time of grief.

Grief can feel like an endless experience with no light at the end of the tunnel. But rest in this promise from God: Grief will not last forever, and your pain will one day turn to joy. Even though you may not see it now, hold on to the hope that comes after grief.

Lord, when my grief is overwhelming, please turn this pain into joy and bring hope from my sorrow. Amen.

Discussion Questions

1. What has been your experience with grief?

_____

_____

_____

2. What has helped you during times of grief? What value do you find in remembering that grief does not last forever?

_____

_____

_____

3. In what ways can you hold on to hope while walking through grief?

_____

_____

_____

Making Things Right

Commentary

Today, we learn more about Peter, one of Jesus's most zealous disciples. Along with James and John, Peter was a part of Jesus's inner circle who witnessed and experienced things the other disciples did not. He would even go on to become a "pillar," or influential figure, in the church (Galatians 2:9).

Prior to his death, Jesus predicted that Peter would deny him. Hearing this, Peter vehemently objected and told Jesus that even if everyone else did, he would never deny him. However, Jesus maintained that before the rooster crowed, Peter would deny him three times.

In our reading, Peter was sitting outside a courtyard when a servant girl approached him. She called him out as one of Jesus's disciples. Because of Peter's previous zeal, we would expect him to proudly say, "Yes, I am!" However, he denied knowing Jesus twice, and on the third time, he even invoked a curse on himself and swore that he didn't know Jesus.

When the rooster crowed, Peter remembered Jesus's words and wept bitterly.

Have you ever messed up badly? The grief we feel after making a terrible mistake is painful. It's important to acknowledge it and confess where we went wrong. However, we should not linger in this kind of grief for too long. This can be crippling and prevent us from doing whatever is needed to make things right and begin healing.

This moment of weakness could have hindered Peter's ministry. However, he received Jesus's forgiveness, made things right, and moved on. While taking time to grieve certain things is important, we must not allow grief to consume us.

Lord, I've messed up badly. Help me walk through my grief but not linger in it for too long. Help me make things right so I can begin healing. Amen.

Discussion Questions

1. Have you ever made a mistake like Peter did?

_____

_____

_____

2. Why do you think we find ourselves consumed by this kind of grief?

_____

_____

_____

3. How can Peter's life encourage you to work on moving beyond your past mistakes?

_____

_____

_____

Forsaken on the Cross

Commentary

Jesus's entire life and ministry on Earth led up to one important moment: his death on the cross. This was a dark and painful day. Jesus hung on the cross all alone. Except for John, his disciples were nowhere to be found. The crowds that followed him wanting to see miracles turned on him and supported his crucifixion. Even more painful, Jesus was forsaken by his Father.

Before his death, Jesus cried out to God from the cross, "*Eli, Eli, lema sabachthani?*" This is Aramaic for "My God, my God, why have you forsaken me?"

Jesus was not the first to use these words. They come from Psalm 22 and express the emotions of King David. As an heir of David, Jesus felt just as David did and more. David experienced pain and rejection and *felt* forsaken by God. However, Jesus experienced death and was truly forsaken by God, even if only for a moment. Writer and theologian Donald Macleod says that when Jesus hung on the cross, "God had closed his ears . . . No word came from heaven to remind him that he was God's Son . . . No angel came to strengthen him."

Have you ever felt the pain of abandonment or rejection? No one wants to feel forsaken. We all want to feel loved and accepted.

The good news is that Jesus was forsaken on the cross *momentarily* so that we could be accepted by God *eternally*. Because of Jesus, we can have confidence that our sorrow will not last forever. He bore the weight of the cross for us so that after our grief, we could experience great joy and hope.

Lord Jesus, thank You for bearing the weight of the cross in my place. Thank You for experiencing grief so that my grief and sorrow do not have to last forever. Amen.

Discussion Questions

1. What do you take away from Jesus's words in Matthew 27:46?

_____

_____

_____

2. Can you relate to Jesus's feelings of abandonment in this moment? What was it like?

_____

_____

_____

3. Do you feel any solidarity from Jesus as you walk through your own grief? How do you feel his support?

_____

_____

_____

Grieving with Hope

Commentary

Each of the Gospels reports women as the first eyewitnesses of Jesus's resurrection. Mark's Gospel explains that Mary Magdalene; Mary, mother of James; and Salome brought spices to anoint Jesus's body and complete his burial preparations. When Mary Magdalene saw that the stone was removed from the entrance of his tomb, she assumed that someone had come and stolen Jesus's body.

After alerting the other disciples who came and saw for themselves, Mary sat outside the tomb, crying. In her mind, Jesus's death was permanent, and now she wouldn't even have the ability to honor his body in death. The grief of the crucifixion was compounded by the grief of physically losing his body.

While she sat there, a man came out and asked her why she was crying. Not recognizing that he was Jesus, she asked where he had taken Jesus's body. However, Jesus simply said to her, "Mary." Instantly, she recognized who was speaking to her. She turned to him and cried out, "Teacher!"

One may wonder why Mary and the other disciples didn't figure out that Jesus had resurrected from the grave. He had hinted at it many times, but they had not understood. This is because ancient Israelites and Jews who lived around this time had no concept of resurrection or an afterlife. If someone died, they were gone forever.

In fact, Jesus's death was the first resurrection that would lead to even more resurrections. The apostle Paul, a devout follower of Jesus, later explained that Christians can grieve with hope. We experience sadness after loss, but we also recognize that Jesus's death and resurrection has made it possible for others after us to resurrect as well. Because of Christ, God will one day wipe away all tears, and there will be no more death, pain, or grief. We look forward to this glorious day!

*Lord, please walk with me through grief. Help
me find comfort in the truth that, one day,
all tears will be wiped from my eyes.*

Discussion Questions

1. How do you relate to Mary in this passage?

_____

_____

_____

2. Have you ever had an experience where your grief was compounded by another painful situation? How did you handle it?

_____

_____

_____

3. Do you believe that you can grieve with hope? Why or why not?

_____

_____

_____

Reflect and Take Action

Weekly Reflection

- Grief is a difficult experience to walk through, but we can only find healing when we allow ourselves to process it instead of avoiding it.

- Grief can lead to hope and healing. Even though it may feel overwhelming, it will not last forever.

- Peter wept bitterly when he remembered Jesus's words and realized that he had denied his Lord as predicted. However, Peter experienced his grief, received forgiveness, and moved on. When we make mistakes, we can follow Peter's example.

- Jesus was forsaken on the cross by God momentarily so we could experience God's love and acceptance eternally.

Activity of the Week

This week, we spoke about the difficulty of grief and the importance of walking through it instead of ignoring it. Whether you are dealing with a painful situation right now or one from the past, take some time to reflect on what you have lost. Don't do this on your own—instead, ask a friend or loved one to walk alongside you and support you as you express your pain to them. Allow your friend to pray with you about the things you have shared. Talking about your grief and being heard can be a cathartic activity. By doing this regularly with someone you trust, you will slowly begin to experience healing and hope from walking through your grief.

WEEK 7

Love

Daily Readings

The Bible teaches us a lot about love. In fact, in the New International Version of scripture, the word "love" appears 686 times! This is because God is love, and he has made us to love. This week, you will encounter some of Jesus's many profound teachings about love. We will discuss the Great Commandment: the call to love God and our neighbors. Next, you will see how Jesus challenges a common misinterpretation held in the first century about love. Many Jewish people at the time thought that God only expected them to love their neighbors. However, he calls us to love our enemies, too.

After this, we will spend some time focusing on God's love for all humanity. We can only love each other properly when we understand the depth of God's love. We will get practical and look at what it means to remain in Jesus's love. Finally, we'll discuss the importance of caring for others as followers of Jesus. After all, the way we care for each other demonstrates how much we love Jesus. Hopefully this week will challenge and inspire you. Putting some of these practices into place may feel uncomfortable at times, especially when it calls on us to love our enemies and show compassion for others whom we might not understand. Just lean on God for the strength you need.

Loving God and Our Neighbors

Commentary

In Mark 12:28, one of the teachers of the law came to Jesus and asked him to explain which of God's commandments was the most important. What a difficult question! There were the Ten Commandments, more than six hundred Jewish laws, and midrash, which interpreted and then turned the Biblical laws into new laws. How could someone pinpoint the greatest of all those laws?

But Jesus was not stumped. He responded by quoting Deuteronomy 6:4–5 and said that loving God with our heart, soul, mind, and strength and loving our neighbor as ourselves is most important.

If you look at the laws in the Old Testament, you will find that each of them can trace its root back to love for God and one's neighbor. Why? Because God is love. Before any humans existed, the Father, Son, and Holy Spirit existed in a loving relationship with one another. God created us so we could share in this love and pass it on to each other.

While loving God and our neighbors is a simple concept, it isn't easy. It would be way easier if everyone was perfect, but none of us are. You might not feel a lot of love when your spouse or partner doesn't help out with the cooking or dishwashing, or when your children misbehave for the hundredth time in one day. Our "neighbors" can be frustrating, can't they? Yet, Jesus still calls us to love them *as ourselves.*

When we're tired and frustrated by the actions of our loved ones, we must remember that despite our many sins, Jesus has never stopped loving *us.* Love is the greatest commandment. It takes practice, and none of us have perfected it yet. However, we can prioritize love and keep making strides toward loving each other better.

Lord, help me love others even when they are difficult to deal with. May I show them the same kind of love that I would want to receive myself. Amen.

Discussion Questions

1. How does Jesus's love for you influence the way you love others?

_____

_____

_____

2. In what ways have you found it difficult to love the people in your life? How can you strengthen your ability to love them?

_____

_____

_____

3. What does it look like to love God with your heart, soul, mind, and strength? How can you practice love toward God by focusing on each of these areas?

_____

_____

_____

DAY 2

Loving Our Enemies

Commentary

Yesterday, we discussed how difficult it can be to love our neighbors when they wrong us or frustrate us. However, it is even more challenging to love our enemies. Jesus calls on us to do this very hard thing.

In today's reading, Jesus corrected a common misunderstanding of the Old Testament. The scripture never said that we should love our neighbors and hate our enemies; people interpreted it incorrectly and came up with that idea. Instead, Jesus told his audience to love their enemies and pray for those who persecute them. This is incredibly hard to do.

In verse 45, Jesus explained that when we love our enemies, we will be children of our Father in heaven. This is because God loves his enemies and is compassionate toward those who hate him. God allows both good and evil people to enjoy the blessing of sunshine and the gift of rain.

As Christian women, we are taught to love all people. Love does not discriminate, nor does it require any barriers based on differences in background, culture, ethnicity, lifestyle, or anything else. Jesus explains that there is no reward in loving only those who love us and showing kindness only toward those who are kind to us. The reward comes from doing the hard thing and loving everyone just as God would.

Maybe right now you are thinking of someone, or even a group of people, who intentionally hurt you. Perhaps it's someone you used to be close to, like a sibling or an ex-partner. It is painful to love someone who has become your enemy. However, the strength to love our enemies is a gift from God. If you ask him, God will open your heart and allow you to love even those who have been unkind or hurtful toward you.

God, I am thankful to know that You love Your enemies, and You are good toward those who hate You. Give me the strength to love my enemies and show compassion to all people as You would.

Discussion Questions

1. What might be some benefits to loving our enemies?

   _____

   _____

   _____

2. How do you feel that failure to love our enemies might impact our relationship with God?

   _____

   _____

   _____

3. Can you think of someone you find difficult to love? How can you follow Jesus's teachings today and love them anyway?

   _____

   _____

   _____

For God So Loved the World

Commentary

Today's reading teaches us so much about the heart and character of God. Because of his love for the world, he gave Jesus, his one and only Son, so that those who believe in him could have eternal life. Jesus spoke these words to Nicodemus, a teacher of the law who was confused about how one could enter God's Kingdom. In John 3:10, Jesus marveled at the fact that Nicodemus, one of Israel's teachers, did not understand salvation.

Jesus's words likely sounded like foolish talk to Nicodemus. The Old Testament and other Jewish writings only spoke about God's love for Israel. Deuteronomy 14:2 stated that the Jews were his chosen people. God's love for the world seemed like a novel and strange idea. However, if you read the Old Testament carefully, you will see that God's ultimate plan was to extend his love and mercy to the entire world.

Many people misunderstand God's character. Perhaps in the past you have heard that God is distant, cold, vengeful, and unfair. Maybe you have felt this way about God yourself. But the truth is, God loves the world. He loves you, no matter where you are or where you have been. All his intentions toward you are good.

Let's look at John 3:17. It explains that God did not send Jesus into the world to condemn it. This means that whoever believes in Jesus is free from condemnation. If you are struggling with the weight of past sins or mistakes, you can entrust Jesus with them and receive freedom.

It's that simple. When you trust in Jesus, he takes the weight of condemnation off your shoulders and places it on himself. Instead of living in condemnation, you become free to live in God's love today and for all eternity.

Lord, thank You for Your great love toward me. Help me trust in Jesus each day and receive freedom from condemnation. Amen.

Discussion Questions

1. How does John 3:16–20 help you understand God's character better?

_____

_____

_____

2. Are there any past sins or mistakes you still carry? What's holding you back from giving them to Jesus?

_____

_____

_____

3. What do you think it looks like to live free from condemnation?

_____

_____

_____

Remaining in Jesus's Love

Commentary

This reading is a part of a larger volume of encouragement from Jesus offered to his disciples shortly before his death. He told them that he loved them with the same kind of pure and perfect love the Father had toward him. The disciples could be confident that, even though Jesus would no longer be with them physically, his love would remain with them forever.

As he encouraged his disciples, he let them know that it was important for them to remain in his love. While the NIV translation of the Bible uses the word "remain" to translate the Greek word μείνατε (*meinate*), the English Standard Version and King James Version translations use the words "abide" and "continue," respectively. Each of these words is important. When we focus on **remaining** in Jesus's love, we are reminded to never leave the safety of his love. However, **abiding** in his love can be reminiscent of being at home or taking up your residence in his love. Finally, **continuing** in Jesus's love is like being spurred to action and encourages us to do something with his love.

Jesus explained that we remain in his love by keeping his commandments. In verse 12, Jesus told his disciples that his command is to love each other as he loved them. They could remain in Jesus's love by showing sacrificial love and kindness to each other.

Have you ever experienced this kind of love from someone else? Maybe you have received kindness from a stranger when you didn't feel you deserved it. Or maybe you have felt the welcoming arms of Jesus through other sisters in Christ who have invited you into their homes or lives. When we receive this kind of love, it's good to pass it on so that others may have the opportunity to receive it, too. This is what it means to remain in Jesus's love.

Father, help me remain, abide, and continue in Jesus's love. May I be moved to act because of His love and pass it on to others around me. Amen.

Discussion Questions

1. Which of the translations of μείνατε (*meinate*) most resonates with you?

_____

_____

_____

2. Are there any barriers in your life keeping you from remaining in Jesus's love? What are they?

_____

_____

_____

3. How can you pass on Jesus's love to others in your life?

_____

_____

_____

Feed His Sheep

Commentary

After Jesus rose from the grave, he appeared to Peter and the disciples while they were out fishing. They had gone back to their lives as they were before meeting Jesus and did not even recognize him when he appeared. You may recall page 78, where we discussed Peter's grief after denying Jesus. Today, we will look at John 21:15–19, where Jesus reinstated Peter after his fall.

After eating breakfast with the disciples, Jesus asked Peter an important question: "Do you love me more than these?" Some scholars believe that Jesus was referring to Peter's profession as a fisherman, while others think that he was speaking of the other disciples. However, the heart of Jesus's question has to do with whether Peter loved Jesus enough to put him before all other things in his life.

Peter responded, "Yes, Lord. You know that I love you." Jesus asked the same question in three different ways. Each time Peter answered affirmatively, Jesus told him, "Feed my sheep."

There is a clear correlation between our love for Jesus and how we take care of others around us. Life can get busy, and most of us have a lot going on. It can be easy to get caught up in our own issues. But by doing so, we often forget to stop and make time for others.

It's true that Peter was going into formal ministry and would be directly "feeding" God's people. However, this same job extends to us. It may look like bringing a meal over to a family who is grieving a loss, or volunteering at church when you'd rather hang out with friends. If you're a mom, it could look like babysitting your neighbor's kids so another tired mom can have a break.

The way in which we love and serve each other says a lot about our love for Jesus. If you love Jesus, the message is: Feed his sheep.

Jesus, thank You for reminding us how important it is to serve others. Help me show You love by helping and supporting others in my community. Amen.

Discussion Questions

1. Can you identify any of Jesus's "sheep" that you need to feed today? Who might they be?

_____

_____

_____

2. What are some things you can do to make room in your schedule for others?

_____

_____

_____

3. If Jesus were to assess your love for him based on your actions toward others, what would he discover?

_____

_____

_____

Reflect and Take Action

Weekly Reflection

- Loving our neighbors takes practice. We won't be perfect at it, but we can prioritize it and make daily strides toward loving our neighbors better.

- It's just as important to love our enemies as it is to love our neighbors. Although this is a difficult task, we can ask God to open our hearts, allowing us to love those who have been unkind or hurtful.

- John 3:16-20 is an important passage about God's heart and character. He loved us so much that he gave his Son, Jesus, so we could have eternal life.

- Once you have received Jesus's love, it is important to remain in it. One way to remain in Jesus's love is by passing it on to others so they can receive it, too.

- Our love for Jesus calls on us to take care of others in our community. This is not just a task for pastors and leaders in ministry; it is for every Christian.

Activity of the Week

Who are the "sheep" in your life that Jesus is calling you to feed? This week, take some time to pray and consider how you can serve someone in your community. God may place someone on your heart, or he might give you a task to complete. It may even feel different or be outside your comfort zone, but you never know how this act of service may help another. God will give you the courage and wisdom you need to serve on his behalf.

WEEK 8

Forgiveness

Daily Readings

Forgiveness is an important theme in scripture. God has forgiven us of many sins, and he asks us to forgive others as well. While Jesus's teachings about forgiveness are difficult to swallow, they are life-transforming. Forgiveness is not just for the other person; it also leads to freedom and joy in our own lives. As with anything else, we need God's power to help us forgive others. The good news is, he has already empowered us to do so.

This week, we will discuss some key truths about forgiveness. We will look at one woman's response to being forgiven of many sins by Jesus. We will also meet an unforgiving servant who, after being released from a great debt, refused to show mercy to a fellow servant. We'll talk about the importance of making things right with each other before offering worship to God and Jesus's power to forgive sins. Finally, we will look at Jesus's response to those who mocked him on the cross and learn how to mirror Jesus's heart toward others.

Forgiven Much

Commentary

Today's reading may feel a little familiar. That is because you previously read a similar story in Matthew 26:6–13. While these two passages are often seen as parallel accounts of the same story, some Bible scholars believe that they are written about two completely different events.

The story you read on page 8 mentions the disciples' dismay at the unnamed woman for "wasting" her perfume. In this story, Simon the Pharisee was surprised that Jesus allowed a sinful woman to touch him. He argued that if Jesus truly was a prophet, he would know that the woman was a sinner.

Jesus responded by telling a short parable. Two people owed money to a lender. One person owed significantly more than the other. Neither could pay the lender back. Out of kindness, the lender forgave both their debts. Jesus asked, "Who will love him more?" Simon responded, "The one with the greater debt."

Jesus pointed out that the woman with many sins came and showed Jesus great honor. She washed and anointed his feet, even though it was Simon's job as the host to do so. Since she was forgiven of many sins, she demonstrated great love toward Jesus. This is important: She was not forgiven *because* of her love. Instead, she loved because she was previously forgiven.

Can you recall the moment when you received Jesus's forgiveness for your sins? Perhaps you've experienced deep love for Jesus that has caused you to pour your heart out to him each day. Or maybe you cannot yet relate to this woman's story. That's okay, too. The good news is that Jesus has extended his forgiveness to you today. Regardless of how much your debt is, you can receive his mercy.

Thank You for the gift of Your forgiveness, Jesus.
Help me receive it daily and, in turn, be motivated
to pour love on You and others. Amen.

Discussion Questions

1. What do you feel kept Simon from understanding the power of forgiveness?

   _____

   _____

   _____

2. Is there anything holding you back from receiving Jesus's forgiveness in all areas of your life?

   _____

   _____

   _____

3. Have you been forgiven of much? How does that change your heart toward Jesus?

   _____

   _____

   _____

The Unforgiving Servant

Commentary

Peter once asked Jesus if seven times was enough to forgive a brother or sister who sinned against him. In Judaism, you were only required to forgive three times. Peter thought that seven times was more than enough. Surprisingly, Jesus responded that seven times was not enough. Instead, Peter was required to forgive seventy-seven times, or in other Bible translations, seven times seventy times.

Jesus told a parable about a servant who owed a great debt to his master. Since he was unable to pay, his master planned to sell him, his wife, and his children to repay the debt. The servant begged for mercy, and the master obliged and let him go.

Later, the same servant went to one of his peers who owed him a small amount of money and demanded to be repaid. He had no mercy on his fellow servant. Eventually, his master found out, expressed anger for his lack of mercy, and threw him in jail. Jesus ended the parable by conveying that those who are unforgiving can expect this kind of treatment from the Father.

This is a hard parable to swallow. You may have been wronged by others and may still be carrying unforgiveness in your heart after what you went through. But think about this: Through Jesus, God has forgiven all our sins. We may not feel this way, but all our sins (even small ones) are a big deal to God. Yet, he forgives us. In turn, he wants us to forgive others, too.

Now, forgiveness does not necessarily involve reconciliation. Sometimes it is wiser not to invite someone who has wronged you back into your life. Forgiveness simply means that you let the person go and relieve them of the responsibility of repaying their debt. It's not always an easy task, but you don't need to walk through it alone. God is with you.

Lord, please help me forgive as
You have forgiven me. Amen.

Discussion Questions

1. What has your experience been with forgiveness, both on the receiving and giving end?

_____

_____

_____

2. Do you think that three times is enough to show forgiveness? Why or why not?

_____

_____

_____

3. Is there someone you struggle to forgive? How can you invite God to walk with you through this process?

_____

_____

_____

Making Things Right

Commentary

In today's reading, Jesus teaches about the importance of being reconciled to our brothers and sisters before offering gifts to God. If we have wronged someone, it's important to make things right again before coming to God in worship.

Jesus's words here seem to be an allusion to Micah 6:6–8. The Jewish people in Micah's day wondered what kind of sacrifices God would accept. They felt they were doing so much, and yet God was not responding. Micah explained that God required them to do justice, love kindness, and walk humbly with God. The sacrifices were important, but not without those three things.

The word "justice" here refers to making something right. Notice that Jesus places a sense of urgency on making things right with a brother or sister. Even in the process of offering a gift to God, if you remember that you've hurt someone else, immediately stop and seek out that person. Confess where you have gone wrong and request their forgiveness.

Perhaps there is someone in your life you need to receive forgiveness from. Be honest about where you have gone wrong. Express genuine remorse. And here is the key: Do what is required to make things right. It could be as simple as picking up dinner for your spouse or partner after bailing on them the night before, or offering to help a girlfriend who has supported you many times. Maybe it has to do with gossip or slander. You may need to go back and correct the hurtful words you've spoken about another person. Perhaps you need to receive forgiveness from a child you spoke harshly to or even an adult child that you weren't there for during childhood. Think about how you can make things right with this person. After making things right, you can go back and offer your gift to God in worship.

Lord, help me recognize my need for forgiveness. Help me make things right so I can offer genuine worship to You. Amen.

Discussion Questions

1. What have you learned from this passage about God's heart toward forgiveness?

_____

_____

_____

2. Why do you think God values practicing justice, showing kindness, and walking in humility over sacrifices?

_____

_____

_____

3. Is there someone you have wronged recently? How can you make things right with this person?

_____

_____

_____

The Power to Forgive Sins

Commentary

In Mark 2, Jesus demonstrated his power to forgive sins. This was quite a big deal. It led some of the teachers of the law to become angry with Jesus, because they thought he was blaspheming. We'll come back to this shortly, but first, let's look at the context behind this passage.

Jesus was preaching in his hometown of Capernaum. So many people gathered in the house that there was no room left for anyone else to enter. A few men came and wanted to bring their paralyzed friend to Jesus. Since they couldn't get through the crowd, they went up to the roof, dug through it, and lowered their friend down to the place where Jesus was standing. Jesus noticed their faith. Instead of saying to the paralyzed man, "Be healed," he said, "Son, your sins are forgiven."

As mentioned before, the teachers of the law were outraged. Since only God could forgive sins, they thought Jesus was blaspheming, or acting offensively toward God. They were wrong. Jesus was able to tell the man, "Your sins are forgiven," because he *was* God. He wasn't blaspheming. He was simply using the authority that rightfully belonged to him.

You may wonder why Jesus mentioned sin when this man needed healing. It's not that his sickness was because of his sin. Instead, he was expressing to the man and the crowd that since he had the power to do the visible miracle of healing, he could also do the invisible miracle of forgiving sins.

Jesus has the power to forgive sins. You no longer need to carry your guilt. Just as this paralyzed man was able to immediately get up and walk, you can get up and walk in freedom from sin, too.

Jesus, thank You for Your forgiveness. Help
me walk in freedom from sin today. Amen.

Discussion Questions

1. Is there anything that stands out to you about Jesus's interaction with the paralyzed man or the assumptions of the teachers of the law?

_____

_____

_____

2. What are some of the sins in your life weighing you down right now?

_____

_____

_____

3. How does the knowledge of Jesus's power to forgive sins impact your life today?

_____

_____

_____

Plant Seeds for the Harvest

Commentary

We learn a lot about Jesus's heart from Luke 23:32–38. As he hung on the cross, people mistreated him and scoffed at him. Roman soldiers stole his clothing and divided the pieces among themselves. He was given vinegar to drink instead of water to quench his thirst.

During Jesus's time on Earth, he went around doing good to everyone (Acts 10:38). He taught people how to connect with and serve the Father better. He fed many hungry people and healed the sick. But as he hung on the cross, he experienced betrayal from the people who previously followed him in crowds wanting to hear his teaching. He was dying for their sins and yet they scoffed at him.

If you were in Jesus's position, would you have forgiveness in your heart? Most of us would probably forfeit our mission and opt to save ourselves. But look at what Jesus said. As he endured pain and suffering for people who did not care, he prayed, "Father, forgive them, for they do not know what they are doing." He chose to die for people who did not love him.

Have you ever had to show kindness toward someone who didn't appreciate it? This could be a partner or colleague, a child or parent, or even a stranger on the street. It's a difficult task. But be encouraged; your kindness shows that you share the heart of Christ. Just as Jesus had compassion for those who sinned against him, you can have compassion for those who take your kindness for granted.

We don't know this for sure, but it's likely that some of those who stood mocking Jesus at the cross may have later become his followers. His sacrifice was not in vain. Likewise, your choice to mirror the heart of Jesus toward others plants a seed that can lead to a wonderful harvest.

Lord, forgive those who take my kindness for granted. Even though the fruit is not yet visible, I believe these seeds I'm planting will lead to a beautiful harvest. Amen.

Discussion Questions

1. How do you respond if you offer kindness to someone who does not appreciate it or who repays you with disdain?

_____

_____

_____

2. Have you witnessed this type of harvest? What was it like?

_____

_____

_____

3. What can you do to encourage yourself as you serve people who aren't appreciative?

_____

_____

_____

Reflect and Take Action

Weekly Reflection

- Regardless of how much debt you have, Jesus extends mercy to you. As you receive his forgiveness, think about how you can demonstrate love toward him.

- Forgiveness does not always require reconciliation. Forgiveness simply means that we let the person who has wronged us go and relieve them of the responsibility of repaying their debt.

- Our relationships matter to Jesus. If we have hurt another person, it is important to make things right quickly.

- The choice to mirror the heart of Jesus toward others and love them, even when they don't appreciate you, plants a seed that can bring a wonderful harvest.

Activity of the Week

This week, you reflected on how Jesus cares about the relationships we have with our brothers and sisters. He cares so much that he tells us to be reconciled to each other before offering worship to God. There might be someone in your life who you need to either forgive or receive forgiveness from. If there is someone you need to forgive, if possible, reach out to them and verbally express your desire to forgive them. In some situations, this may not be possible, but you can still say a prayer of forgiveness. On the other hand, if there is someone you need to receive forgiveness from, reach out to them, confess where you went wrong, and do what is needed to make things right.

Prayer and Fasting

Daily Readings

Prayer and fasting are spiritual disciplines that draw us closer to God. The fourteenth-century reformer Martin Luther noted that to be a Christian without prayer is no more possible than to be alive without breathing. While prayer can feel daunting for many Christians, it is simply a conversation with God. Although he knows all things, he wants to connect with us. He cares about your needs and wants to hear about your day.

This week, we'll discover some of Jesus's teachings on prayer. He gives us a model that can help us with our prayers. We can use this model to honor God and draw closer to him as we pray. We will also look at Zechariah's prayer and the parable of the persistent widow. Each of these stories can teach us something meaningful about prayer and be a helpful guide for us as we grow in our prayer lives.

While fasting involves giving up food, it also involves spending time with God, similar to prayer. This week, we'll look at why Christians fast. Learning how to pray and fast is like training at the gym. While it can feel difficult at first, it gets easier over time. These teachings from Jesus will help you grow in your practice of prayer and fasting.

Zechariah's Prayer

Commentary

Today we read Luke 1:11–17, where we encounter Zechariah, the father of Jesus's cousin, John the Baptist. Zechariah was a priest in Israel. This means he bore the responsibility of praying to God on behalf of the nation. It was Zechariah's turn to go into the most sacred part of the temple and burn incense to God. While Zechariah was inside the temple, everyone else was praying outside. Since the burning of incense symbolized prayer and communion with God, the hour of incense was likely a designated time for people to pray.

Based on verse 13, we can infer that Zechariah was not only praying for the nation; he also had a personal petition that he offered to God. He and his wife Elizabeth were struggling with infertility. They really wanted a son but were unable to conceive.

While Zechariah prayed, an angel came to him and let him know that his prayer was answered. Elizabeth would have a son named John. He would be a special child who would help reunite parents and their children and prepare all of Israel for the coming of the Lord.

What is it that you are praying for today? Maybe you desire to have a child like Zechariah and Elizabeth did. Or perhaps there is another pressing concern on your heart. Just as the angel reminded Zechariah that God heard his prayer, please know that God hears yours, too. We don't know how long Zechariah and Elizabeth were praying. It could have been many years. However, one day when they probably least expected it, God answered their prayers. Keep on praying and keep believing that God will answer you, too.

*Lord, please give me the strength to keep praying
for this need that is on my heart. Even though I
don't have my answer yet, may I always remember
that You hear me and You will answer. Amen.*

Discussion Questions

1. What do you ask of God in your prayers?

2. If you were Zechariah, how would you have felt when the angel
   told you that your prayers were answered?

3. What part of this passage can you use as encouragement to keep
   praying? What stands out about the words that moves you?

Pray Like This

Commentary

Jesus began this teaching by explaining how *not* to pray, and then he gave his audience a model for how they can properly pray to God. He told them that they should not pray like the hypocrites who stand in synagogues and on street corners wanting to be seen by others. The Greek word that "hypocrites" derived from originally referred to actors who wore different masks when playing various roles. While acting on stage for entertainment is good, acting in our spiritual life is not helpful at all.

Jesus explained that prayer should be private; when you pray, go into your room, close the door, and pray to God, who is unseen. God openly rewards those who pray in private.

Now, this doesn't mean not to ever pray publicly or in a group setting with others. Jesus simply warned about prayer motivated by the opportunity to be seen and applauded by others.

Jesus also commented on the prayers offered by members of pagan religions. They would say the names of their gods repeatedly, expecting to receive an answer (see 1 Kings 18:25 and Acts 19:34, for example). Jesus warned his listeners to avoid praying in that way. It's not simply about not repeating God's name; it's more about having depth and meaning to one's prayer.

Jesus gives his audience a model for how to pray. It begins with an invocation—another word for the process of calling out to God for help—and then includes six specific petitions. The first three focus on God's holiness, God's Kingdom, and God's will. The last three focus on personal needs.

If you struggle with prayer, try using this example as a model. As you continue to pray to God, it will get easier. Remember that the Holy Spirit, who is within you, will help you.

Lord, help me offer sincere prayers to You. As I practice praying daily, may I grow closer to You. Amen.

Discussion Questions

1. Do you find prayer to be challenging? What are some of your greatest challenges when it comes to prayer?

_____

_____

_____

2. If you are a mother or caregiver, how do you teach your children about prayer? Where do you use it together?

_____

_____

_____

3. Have you experienced God's open reward from time praying in private? What was it like?

_____

_____

_____

DAY 3

The Persistent Widow

Commentary

In Luke 18, Jesus told a parable about a persistent widow and an unjust judge. This judge did not fear God, nor did he care about the thoughts or opinions of others. He was only focused on himself and did not prioritize justice. However, this persistent widow kept coming to the judge asking for justice against her enemy. He refused her requests for a long time. Eventually, he granted her request because he didn't want her to keep bothering him or to potentially attack him.

Because of her persistence, this widow received justice from a judge who had no intention of helping anyone but himself.

Jesus told his audience that if the unjust judge brought about justice because of this widow's persistence, God, who is just and loves his people, will certainly hear their persistent prayers. God cares and doesn't want to see his people suffer in pain. He hears their cries and sees their tears. As Jesus mentioned, God will see that they get justice quickly.

Now, from our human perspective, God's quick justice may seem slow. We may be praying for years for God to fix what's wrong in our lives and communities. We may be dealing with injustices that come from being a woman, a mother, a daughter, or a human. It may feel frustrating. But God's timing is not like ours, and even though justice seems to be delayed, he will come and make things right.

Do you feel like this widow did? Perhaps you've been treated poorly by others, or maybe life is just pretty hard for you right now. Maybe you've been crying out to God to help you, and you're on the verge of giving up. Don't give up. Keep praying to God. He hears your prayers, and he will come and make things right.

Lord, when there's a lot going wrong in my life, please come and make things right. As I wait, give me the strength to keep praying and trusting in You. Amen.

Discussion Questions

1. Do you see God as a just or unjust judge? Why?

_____

_____

_____

2. Why do you think God's quick justice often seems slow to us?

_____

_____

_____

3. How can you remind yourself to remain persistent even when you've been praying for years?

_____

_____

_____

DAY 4

Why Do We Fast?

Commentary

Christian fasting involves giving up food or other items for a short while to spend more time with God. Fasting during Jesus's day was practiced for many reasons, including to express sorrow, repentance, or humility or to prepare oneself to serve God. In Mark 2:18–20, some people came to Jesus and asked why his disciples were not fasting while John's disciples and the Pharisees were fasting.

The law only required fasting on the Day of Atonement; however, during the first century, many Jews observed four other yearly fasts. Strict Pharisees fasted twice a week. Everyone else observed many fasts, but Jesus's disciples seemed to barely ever be fasting.

Jesus responded to this question with another: "How can the guests of a bridegroom fast while he is with them?" It would have been considered rude to fast at a wedding or celebration. Jesus was getting at the fact that he was the proverbial bridegroom, and that since the disciples were in his presence, they were already having direct fellowship with God. As such, fasting was not necessary for them.

However, one day, Jesus's disciples would need to fast. Jesus would not always be physically present with them. This is the same reason we fast today. It's how we express our eagerness for Jesus to return and correct all that is broken in the world. When we fast, we remember Jesus's sacrifice by making our own sacrifices as well.

We won't always need to fast. But until Jesus returns, it is good to have seasons of fasting and reflection. Have you or someone you know experienced deep pain or sorrow? Do you turn on the news and witness the evil in the world? This is when it is good to fast and cry out to Jesus in prayer to return and fix what is going wrong.

*Jesus, I know that You are returning one day
to fix the pain and evil in the world. Help me
fast at appropriate times as a reminder of
my longing for You to come back. Amen.*

Discussion Questions

1. What do you notice about the Pharisees from today's reading?

_____

_____

_____

2. Do you take time to fast during specific seasons? Why or
   why not?

_____

_____

_____

3. How can fasting remind you of Jesus's sacrifice?

_____

_____

_____

Prayer and Fasting

Commentary

In Mark 9:25–29, Jesus cast an impure spirit out of a young boy. For more context on this story, see page 50, where we discussed Matthew's account of the event. Instead of focusing on faith as Matthew did, Mark's account highlights prayer and fasting.

After the impure spirit came out of the boy, the disciples asked why they hadn't been able to drive it out. Jesus responded and said that this kind of spirit could only be cast out by prayer and fasting. Some translations (like the NIV) only say "prayer," while others mention "prayer and fasting."

The disciples were right in wondering why they couldn't drive out the demon. Jesus had previously given them authority over evil spirits, and they had driven out demons prior to this event (see Mark 6:7 and 6:13). Yet, when this young boy needed help, they were unable to help him.

Some believe that when Jesus said "this kind" can only come out by prayer and fasting, he was referring to a specific kind of demon. However, it's more likely that Jesus is speaking of demonic spirits in general. The disciples would not be able to drive out such evil spirits without these tools.

Prayer and fasting are ways that we connect with God. The power to drive out demons does not come from one's own ability or merit. It comes from a connection to God. You may not be driving out too many demons on your Christian journey. However, you may have had very difficult situations in life. You can only have success against those situations by being in close connection with God. A life that includes prayer and fasting will help you as you go through these kinds of experiences.

Lord, help me develop a stronger prayer life and a deeper connection to You so I can have success against the spiritual warfare I experience in life. Amen.

Discussion Questions

1. If you had to assess your prayer life, how would you describe it?

_____

_____

_____

2. What are some difficult situations in your life that don't seem to go away?

_____

_____

_____

3. How do you think a close connection with God can help you with these situations?

_____

_____

_____

Reflect and Take Action

Weekly Reflection

- What is it that you are praying for today? Just as God heard Zechariah and Elizabeth's prayer, God hears yours, too.

- Avoid praying like the Pharisees and the members of pagan religions. Instead, follow the model of prayer Jesus gives us in Matthew 6:5–13.

- The unjust judge granted the persistent widow her request because she wouldn't stop asking. Pray persistently. God, who is just, hears you and will grant your request.

- Fasting is important for Christians. There is a time to fast and a time to rejoice.

- The power to overcome spiritual opposition does not come from your ability or merit. It comes from the deep connection with God that we develop through prayer and fasting.

Activity of the Week

This week, we spoke about prayer and fasting. Maybe you have never fasted, or perhaps you haven't done it in a long time. Let's practice fasting this week. You don't have to start out by fasting from food. Instead, you may want to choose something else that is difficult to give up. It could be sugar, social media, or a streaming service. Choose a day or two to give up the item you chose and spend that time with God instead. While fasting, it is helpful to pray as well. Pray a little more than you usually would on this day. You can also meditate on scripture and listen to music that draws you closer to God.

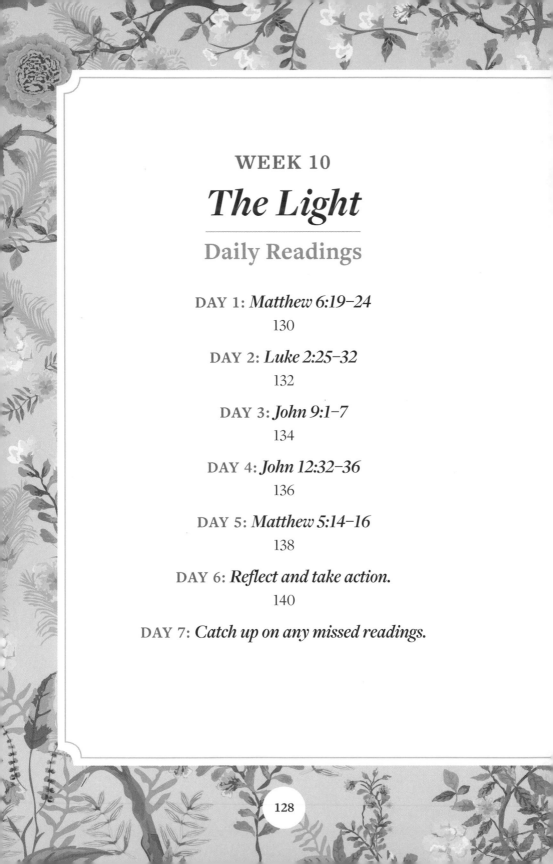

The Light

Daily Readings

Light and darkness are mentioned often in the Gospels. The bad news is that there is darkness in the world. This darkness can feel overwhelming at times. It is difficult to see the pain that darkness causes for our friends and loved ones. But the good news is that there is also light. The light is much greater than the darkness. In fact, John 1:5 explains that the light shines in darkness and the darkness cannot overcome it.

This week, we will discuss the lamp of your body and how healthy choices bring light to your entire body. We will learn about Jesus's role as the light that points Gentiles toward God. We'll also discover why it is significant that Jesus is the light of the world. We will see how, as the light of the world, Jesus brings healing and freedom to those who encounter him. He also enables us to be lights in this world, pointing others to him.

Ultimately, light will always triumph over darkness. As you study this week, think about how you can participate in shining a light in your own community. Prayerfully consider what God is asking you to do with your light and make a commitment to do just that.

The Lamp of the Body

Commentary

In today's reading, Jesus warned his audience against storing up their treasures on Earth rather than in heaven. He mentioned that one's eyes are the lamp of the body, and that if one's eyes are unhealthy, it leads to darkness in their life. He goes on to explain how important it is to serve only one master: God or money.

Each of the smaller sections within this passage seems to stand on its own, and some readers may wonder how they relate to each other. However, Jesus is communicating to his audience how they are to live their personal lives as members of God's Kingdom.

Verse 21 explains that one's heart will be where their treasure is. This leads into verses 22 and 23, because the heart and the eye represented both one's convictions and course of life in Jewish culture. Jesus was explaining that if someone's life choices and convictions were healthy, their lives would be full of light. However, if their choices were unhealthy, their lives would be full of darkness.

The eye is just one small part of the body, and yet it determines whether we are in darkness or in light. We take in ideas, beliefs, and thought patterns through our eyes. The things we see and experience each day can impact how we live our lives.

Let's look at social media. It is a huge space often used for the transfer of ideas. There are positive and negative ideas. While we don't need to avoid social media entirely, we should be discerning of what ideas we choose to take in. Too many negative ideas can bring darkness into our lives. It can lead us away from our relationship with God and dim our relationships with others and ourselves. Instead of consuming negative things, God wants us to fill our eyes with goodness so we will be full of light. This light illuminates our path, as well as that of our family, friends, and those around us.

Lord, help me be mindful of what I consume so my life will continue to be full of light instead of darkness. Amen.

Discussion Questions

1. In your opinion, how can storing treasures on Earth lead to unhealthy eyes? Is there a connection between the two?

_____

_____

_____

2. What happens in your life when you are consuming negative ideas? What about positive ideas?

_____

_____

_____

3. How can you use resources like social media in a way that honors God and brings his goodness into your life?

_____

_____

_____

Light for the Gentiles

Commentary

In Luke 2, we encounter Simeon, a devout man who received a promise from the Holy Spirit that one day he would see God's Messiah. Simeon was waiting for the consolation of Israel that was prophesied by Isaiah many years earlier. Isaiah mentioned that God would comfort his people and forgive their sins.

Simeon went into the temple, and while he was there, Jesus's parents brought him inside for the Jewish rite of circumcision. As soon as Simeon held baby Jesus in his arms, he realized that he was holding the Messiah and he praised God.

Notice that in verses 30–32, Simeon mentioned that his "eyes have seen [God's] salvation . . . a light for revelation to the Gentiles, and the glory of your people Israel." He was describing Jesus as this light for the Gentiles. Scripture explains that the Gentiles were in darkness. Jesus was the light who came so they could see God's revelation—that is, his existence and love for them—clearly. Jesus also came as the glory of Israel. They already had God's revelation and would now be the people that the Messiah would come through. Jesus came so that people who did not know God could have an opportunity to see him clearly.

Perhaps you feel that you do not have God's revelation. Maybe you've struggled to understand scripture or connect with God in prayer and worship. Jesus brings this revelation so that you can truly know God. Turn to him and allow him to light your way so that you can see the beauty of God's truth clearly.

Lord, thank You for being the light that helps me see God's revelation. Sometimes I struggle to understand, but I believe that You will help me each day. Amen.

Discussion Questions

1. What do you think it looks like for someone to truly know God?

_____

_____

_____

2. Have you ever felt like you were in darkness and could not see clearly? What was it like?

_____

_____

_____

3. How have Jesus, his teachings, and these readings helped you see God more clearly?

_____

_____

_____

Doing God's Work While It Is Day

Commentary

In John 9, Jesus encountered a man who was born blind. Curious, Jesus's disciples asked if someone's sin was the reason for this man's condition. Jesus responded that sin is not always the cause of someone's suffering. Sometimes God allows people to go through hardship so he can show them his mercy and power by freeing them from their suffering.

In John 9:4, Jesus explained that since it is "day," they must do God's work. He is referring to verses 1–3 and the miracle he performed when he healed the blind man. When Jesus says "day" and "night," he is speaking metaphorically. The "day" is the time he spent on Earth with his disciples. It was the opportunity to teach, heal, and do good work for those on Earth. Since Jesus is the light of the world, the "night" came after his death, when he was no longer with his disciples.

Jesus wanted his disciples to understand that he would not physically be with them forever. There was work God wanted them to do while Jesus was still on Earth. They needed to make good use of their time by doing that work diligently. They had his light with them to guide them as they worked.

Likewise, each of us has work that God calls us to do. Maybe you are a teacher or a volunteer at a local shelter. Perhaps you are searching for a new career or more ways to do God's work. Perhaps you serve at your local church. Maybe you are a mom raising Christian children. Right now, it is day and you can do God's work. However, it won't always be day. By doing God's work diligently while it is day, when you can no longer work, you can confidently say that you have done your best.

Jesus, help me recognize the work God is calling me to do and help me make the most of the opportunity I have to serve others. Amen.

Discussion Questions

1. What kind of work is God calling you to do? If you're not sure, what are some steps you can take to help you figure it out?

_____

_____

_____

2. Do you feel that you are making the most of your opportunity to do God's work?

_____

_____

_____

3. How does knowing that Jesus is a guiding light for you direct or motivate you as you work?

_____

_____

_____

DAY 4

Children of Light

Commentary

In today's reading, Jesus spoke about his death to the crowd listening. He told them that he would be lifted from Earth and would draw all kinds of people to himself. This was to show the crowd that he would die on a cross.

People from the crowd questioned what Jesus had to say. Since law said that the Messiah would remain forever, how would he be "lifted up" in death? They couldn't understand that one day the Messiah would die.

Jesus explained that he would be with them for only a little while longer. After that, they would no longer experience his physical presence. Notice that Jesus describes himself as "the light" here. We mentioned yesterday that Jesus is the light of the world. He tells his audience to walk while they have the light before darkness comes and overtakes them. "Walking" refers to how someone lives and conducts themselves. As the light, Jesus helped his people live and conduct themselves as God wanted them to.

In verse 36, Jesus also explained that they should believe in the light. By doing so, they would become children of light. This is key. Although Jesus was going away, if they believed in him, they could become children of light and would be able to live as God called them to live, even when Jesus was no longer physically present.

Even though we live in a dark world without Jesus's physical presence, there is hope for us. Since you believe in him, you are a child of light. Jesus gives you the ability to be a light and to live in light each day. When you feel overwhelmed by darkness around you, remember that you can be a light for those experiencing darkness. As a child of light, you point others to Jesus, who is the even greater light and leads them out of darkness.

Lord, help me be a light to those in darkness
and point them to You. Amen.

Discussion Questions

1. Do you see yourself as a child of light? Why or why not?

   _____

   _____

   _____

2. What do you feel God is calling you to do with your light to help others in darkness? How are you helping (or how can you help) the children in your life shine their own light?

   _____

   _____

   _____

3. What from today's reading can encourage you when you are overwhelmed by the darkness around you?

   _____

   _____

   _____

We Are the Light

Commentary

In Matthew 5, Jesus went up to the top of a mountain and began to give a sermon. We know it today as the Sermon on the Mount. It recalls a similar sermon given by the patriarch Moses to the Israelites as they were about to leave Mount Horeb. They were about to enter the Promised Land, and Moses wanted them to be prepared for what lay ahead. Their lives would help others see the beauty and greatness of God.

Likewise, in the Sermon on the Mount, Jesus was preparing his listeners for a new Promised Land that they would soon enter. Instead of going to a physical place, they were preparing to enter the spiritual Kingdom of God. In fact, this Kingdom would be coming to Earth, and they would be the ones responsible for carrying it to the entire world. It was an important task, but one that Jesus would be guiding them through every step of the way.

Have you ever found it difficult to be a light to others? It can be a challenge to be a light within our communities. However, as Jesus mentioned, a town built on a hill cannot be hidden. It's meant to attract visitors to itself. A lamp is meant to shine brightly and guide those struggling through the darkness. Ultimately, Jesus says, "let your light shine before others" so they can see your good deeds and glorify the Father.

We are meant to point others to our good and gracious Father. When they see our good deeds, they will naturally think of how good God is. Even Jesus's own life glorified the Father. He brought glory to God by doing God's work on Earth (John 17:4). May our lights shine as well, and may we glorify God through the things we do. No matter our roles in the world, we can impact those who surround us and help their lights shine brighter, too.

Lord, help me shine my light even when
it's hard. May my light help guide others
so they can glorify You. Amen.

Discussion Questions

1. How does today's reading help you in your role as a light to the world?

_____

_____

_____

2. What do you feel is most challenging about shining your light in a dark world? Most inspirational?

_____

_____

_____

3. What are some ways you can fulfill your role of being a light within your community today?

_____

_____

_____

Reflect and Take Action

Weekly Reflection

- The ideas, beliefs, and thought patterns we take in each day can impact how we live our lives. We want to be discerning of what ideas we choose to take in.

- Jesus is the light of the world. He came so that people who did not know God could have an opportunity to see him clearly.

- We have work that God calls us to do. Right now, it is day and we can do God's work. By working diligently now, when we can no longer work, we will be able to confidently say that we have done our best.

- There is hope for us in a dark world, even without Jesus's physical presence. Since we believe in him, we are children of light.

- Jesus allows us to be lights in the world to guide others to him. We use our gifts so others may see our good deeds and glorify God.

Activity of the Week

Now that you have learned about and reflected on what it means to be the light of the world, let's put it into action. One way to shine your light in the world is by being present and noticing the people around you. Is there a woman you can help by shining your light? This week, take some time and get to know someone new in your community. Ask the Lord to help you find this woman. Strike up a conversation, and if there is an opportunity, invite her to coffee or lunch so you can get to know her more. You never know how God can use this simple gesture to remind someone of his love through your light.

WEEK 11

Doubt

Daily Readings

Many people struggle with doubt in their Christian journey. If this is something you struggle with, too, relax and take a deep breath. You are not alone. In fact, doubt can help strengthen your faith if you approach it in the right way. This week, we're going to explore what Jesus teaches about doubt. By the end of the week, you'll have resources and practical help for understanding and dealing with your doubt.

First, we will look at how doubt can manifest in the lives of even strong believers. You'll encounter John the Baptist, his struggle with doubt, and Jesus's response.

Next, you will see Jesus's disciples in a moment of doubt after his death and how Jesus was patient with them when they doubted. We will learn about Peter and his experience walking on water. Although Jesus did not want Peter to doubt, he still reached out and rescued him when he did. We will look at Jesus's teachings about a withered fig tree and what they mean for our doubts. Finally, we will meet the apostle nicknamed "doubting Thomas" and learn about his struggle with doubt.

You Really Are the One

Commentary

In Matthew 11:1–6, John the Baptist questioned whether Jesus truly was the Messiah. John the Baptist was Jesus's cousin and the son of Zechariah and Elizabeth. He was called to be the forerunner of Jesus, meaning that his ministry prepared the Jewish people to receive Jesus as their Messiah. John was a passionate preacher of the Good News and spent his days baptizing people who came to him. By all accounts, he didn't appear to be much of a doubter.

However, in this passage, John was in prison. Herod Antipas, the corrupt king appointed by the Romans to lead the Jews, locked him away and took control of his fate. In a moment of doubt, John asked, "Are you the one who is to come, or should we expect someone else?" John had strong faith, and yet he still ended up wrestling with doubt.

Maybe you're in a similar place. You've been on fire for Jesus, and you have done so many great things for him. But perhaps something happened that changed everything in your life. You're wondering, *Is Jesus truly who he says he is?*

Doubt happens. Even the strongest believers doubt sometimes. Don't be afraid to turn to Jesus with your doubts and questions. He wants to support you through the process.

Jesus responded to John's doubts by pointing out all the signs that he was the Messiah: The blind received their sight, the lame could walk, those with leprosy were cleansed, the deaf heard, the dead were raised, and the poor heard the Good News.

Sometimes when you wrestle with doubt, you just need to look around and notice the signs. Remembering all that Jesus has done will strengthen your faith and help sustain you through the moments of doubt.

Jesus, I am grateful that You are with me in my doubt. Please give me the strength to keep believing that You are who You say You are. Amen.

Discussion Questions

1. Have you ever doubted Jesus? What happened?

_____

_____

_____

2. What are some signs in your life that remind you of who Jesus is?

_____

_____

_____

3. How might it comfort you to know that even the strongest believers sometimes doubt?

_____

_____

_____

When Doubts Rise

Commentary

After Jesus's resurrection, he appeared to his disciples, but they had doubts that the person they saw was really him. In Luke 24:36, Jesus greeted his disciples by saying, "Peace be with you." Instead of recognizing Jesus, they were startled and afraid. They were convinced they had seen a ghost. Jesus responded by asking two simple questions: "Why are you troubled? Why do doubts rise in your minds?"

Then he invited them to look at his hands and feet. He wanted them to recognize the scars from the nails where he had been pierced on the cross. Surely the disciples would know it was Jesus because of his scars. Next, he told them to touch him and see that he was truly Jesus. If he were a ghost, he would not have flesh and bones that could be touched.

Why didn't the disciples recognize Jesus? First, they could not wrap their minds around the reality of Jesus's resurrected body. Second, they were unsure that resurrection was even a possibility. Although Jesus had told them that he would rise from the dead, they didn't understand. So, when they encountered him after his death, they were afraid and doubtful that it was really him.

Remember that Jesus was gentle with his disciples in their doubt. While he wanted them to believe, he was also willing to show them again and again. Just as Jesus was patient with them, he is also patient with you in your journey. Eventually these doubting disciples became confident messengers of Jesus and proclaimed his truth to the world. As doubts arise, simply ask him to remind you of the truth that he has spoken to you. Like the disciples, you will one day overcome your doubt, and hopefully you, too, will become a messenger of truth to the world—to your children, if and when you are a parent, and to others walking in the Christian faith.

Lord, thank You for being patient with me in my doubt. Please help me overcome doubt and believe. Amen.

Discussion Questions

1. How do you think you would have responded if you were one of the disciples Jesus appeared to?

   _____

   _____

   _____

2. Have any doubts arisen in your heart as you've read today's passage? What are they?

   _____

   _____

   _____

3. What are some doubts you've already overcome in your life? If you are a mother or caregiver, how have you responded to your children's questions about God's existence?

   _____

   _____

   _____

DAY 3

Why Did You Doubt?

Commentary

Matthew 14:28–33 is a well-known passage in the Gospels. We've already met Peter, one of Jesus's most zealous and passionate disciples. After the feeding of the five thousand, Jesus had his disciples get into a boat ahead of him and journey toward the other side of the lake while he took time to dismiss the crowd. After this, Jesus went up a mountain to pray. Right before dawn, Jesus went to meet his disciples. Instead of taking a boat, he walked on the water toward them. Naturally, the disciples were terrified when they saw Jesus. But confidently, Peter said, "Jesus, if it's you, allow me to walk out on the water to meet you."

This is how Matthew 14:28 begins. Jesus invited Peter to come, and he got out of the boat and walked toward Jesus. He was doing fine for a while, but then he noticed the wind, became afraid, and started to sink. As Jesus reached out and saved Peter, he asked, "You of little faith, why did you doubt?"

Christian author Dr. Jeannine K. Brown explains that "little faith" is a faith that does not hold firm amid difficult circumstances. "Doubt" in this passage comes from the Greek word *distazo*, which speaks of wavering faith.

While this was not the best response from Peter, it's a completely human one. Sometimes, like Peter, we step out of the boat confidently, but then we're met by life's circumstances and begin to doubt. Jesus's desire is for us to continue to have strong faith in him despite our circumstances. But getting to the place where we have that kind of faith can be a journey. The goal is that one day we can trust Jesus through difficult things without wavering in our faith. Thankfully, Jesus is right there to help us in this journey.

Lord, please strengthen me so when difficult circumstances come, I will not waver in my faith. Amen.

Discussion Questions

1. Can you relate to Peter in this situation? Why or why not?

2. What difficult circumstances are you facing right now? Are they causing you to doubt?

3. How do you think your faith can be strengthened so it doesn't waver?

Take Uncertainties to God

Commentary

Heading from the temple toward the city of Jerusalem, Jesus saw a fig tree on the road. Since he was hungry, he went up to it, expecting fruit, but found nothing except leaves on it. Jesus cursed the tree, and immediately, it withered.

His disciples were amazed at what he did and asked how it happened. Jesus responded that if they had faith and did not doubt, they would be able to do even more than what he did to the fig tree. If they believed in him, they would receive what they asked for in prayer.

Earlier, in Matthew 17:20, Jesus explained how important faith was for his followers. It was necessary for them to have faith because without it, they would not have been able to do any of the things God wanted them to do.

As humans, the disciples were naturally inclined to doubt what they could not understand. They may have wondered how Jesus's words could have caused a fig tree to instantly wither. Jesus wanted them to believe that nothing was impossible with God.

Notice that Jesus said, "If you have faith *and do not doubt.*" He often contrasts faith and doubt. Interestingly, he never compares doubt with certainty. He doesn't expect us to have all the answers. Instead, he wants us to trust God, even when we are unsure.

Have you ever felt uncertain about your future? Maybe you're graduating from college and you aren't sure if you will find the right job, or perhaps you are getting married or having a child and you wonder if you will be a good spouse or parent. Maybe you're planning to move, change jobs, or retire but don't know what your future holds for you. Instead of doubting, have faith by taking those uncertainties to God and believe that nothing is impossible for him.

Jesus, I want to thank You for establishing that faith does not necessarily equal certainty. Help me take my uncertainties to You instead of doubting. Amen.

Discussion Questions

1. Do you agree that there is a difference between faith and certainty? Why or why not?

_____

_____

_____

2. What are some things you currently feel uncertain about?

_____

_____

_____

3. How can you keep your uncertainties from turning into doubt?

_____

_____

_____

Doubting Thomas

Commentary

"Doubting Thomas" is a nickname given to Thomas, one of Jesus's disciples, because of his struggle to believe that Jesus had truly resurrected from the dead. Let's look at his story in John 20:24–29. Prior to this passage, Jesus had appeared to the other disciples, but Thomas was not there. The disciples told Thomas that they had seen Jesus. He replied, "Unless I see the nails . . . and put my hands into his side, I will not believe." He refused to take their word that Jesus, whom he knew had died, was alive again.

A week later, all the disciples, including Thomas, were gathered in a house. Jesus came through the locked doors and greeted them. Then he turned to Thomas and encouraged him to touch his hands and his side where the scars of the crucifixion remained.

Thomas then recognized Jesus and believed. Jesus responded, "Blessed are those who have not seen and still believe."

Was Thomas wrong for wanting to see Jesus before believing? Not at all. Thomas wanted to see the same evidence the other disciples got to see before believing. Although Jesus implored Thomas to stop doubting and believe, he only said this after providing evidence that he truly had resurrected.

While many Christians often interpret verse 29 as a rebuke against Thomas, it isn't. John, who wrote his Gospel sixty to eighty years after Jesus's death, included this statement to encourage his readers who have not seen Jesus to still believe in him.

Like Thomas, you may have had seasons in your life where you've struggled to believe in Jesus. He isn't judging you because you are struggling. Instead, he provides evidence to help you see who he is. He gently walks with you and helps you turn your doubt into faith.

Lord, when I am struggling in my faith and feel consumed by doubt, help me see the evidence of who You are and believe. Amen.

Discussion Questions

1. Do you think it's important to have evidence for your faith? Why or why not?

_____

_____

_____

2. What can you learn from Thomas's reaction to the other disciples' words in John 20:25?

_____

_____

_____

3. If you are struggling in your faith, what kind of evidence do you need from Jesus to help you believe? If you are a mother or caregiver, how can you approach this issue with a questioning child?

_____

_____

_____

Reflect and Take Action

Weekly Reflection

- John the Baptist had strong faith in Jesus and still wrestled with doubt. This can happen to the best of us, so don't be afraid to turn to Jesus with your doubts and questions.

- When doubts arise in your heart, ask Jesus to remind you of the scripture and the truth he has spoken to you.

- Jesus will help you in your journey toward strengthening your faith and trusting him despite any doubts you may have.

- The opposite of doubt is not certainty. Jesus doesn't expect us to have all the answers.

- If you are going through a season of life where you struggle to believe in Jesus, allow him to walk with you and help turn your doubt into faith.

Activity of the Week

When you struggle with doubt, you may find that honest prayers help remind you of the truth. Find a quiet place and take some time to sit in God's presence. As you sit, name your doubts out loud or write them down on paper. Learning to name the things you struggle with is important for developing your Christian faith. However, be patient and allow the Holy Spirit to bring them to mind. After acknowledging a doubt you have, ask God to help you overcome it. Ask him to give you clarity and guide you toward the truth. Keep doing this with each doubt you recall.

Christian Hospitality

Daily Readings

As Christians, we are rarely taught about hospitality, even though it is one of the most important parts of our faith. Jesus calls us to welcome others because this is exactly what he has done for us. When we show radical love and hospitality toward others, we invite them in to be a part of God's family.

Think about a time in your life when someone was particularly welcoming toward you, either in your childhood, your teen years, or adulthood. It may have impacted you greatly. Most people want to have a sense of belonging. This is often why people join groups, organizations, and other communities. When we show hospitality to someone else, we tell them that they belong. Hospitality communicates a powerful message.

This week, we will look at some important passages in the Gospel about hospitality. Some things we will discuss include Jesus's heart toward the "least of these" and the parable of the Good Samaritan.

Some of his words surrounding the topic may feel inspiring and encouraging, while others may seem surprising. As you read, pay attention to what stands out to you about Christian hospitality. Consider your own sense of belonging as a woman in your home, community, workplace, school, or wherever you spend your time. Think about how you can mirror Jesus's teachings in your own life as you interact with your neighbors.

Inviting Others In

Commentary

When you host an event, do you typically invite friends and family, or do you invite people you don't know? You may agree that it feels more normal to invite friends and family to a special event. However, in today's reading, Jesus taught the opposite. Let's look at the context behind Luke 14:7–14.

Jesus was invited to eat in the house of a prominent Pharisee. He noticed that the other guests picked the best seats at the table. He told them a parable and encouraged them to practice humility rather than pridefully exalting themselves.

Then in verse 12, Jesus told his host that when hosting a luncheon or dinner, they should not invite their friends, family, and wealthy neighbors. After all, those people have the means of repaying you when they host their own event in the future. Instead, he said, invite those who are poor, crippled, lame, and blind.

Notice that in verse 14, Jesus told his audience that they would be "repaid at the resurrection of the righteous." This means that God will repay you for your kindness and good works toward his people when Jesus returns. However, he doesn't want us to be motivated to show hospitality because we may be repaid. Instead, we should want to do it because of Jesus's hospitality toward us.

You may know what it feels like to be uninvited; perhaps, as you read this, you are realizing that you have excluded others from events and celebrations. Christian hospitality looks like inviting and welcoming people who would otherwise not be welcomed. When you honor those who cannot honor you back, you demonstrate Christian love. Through Jesus, God has welcomed you into his family, and because of that, it is important to do the same for others.

Lord, thank You for welcoming me into Your family.
Please help me, in turn, welcome others, not for a
reward, but because of my gratitude toward You. Amen.

Discussion Questions

1. Have you ever felt excluded by others? How did it feel?

_____

_____

_____

2. How have you experienced God's hospitality in your own life?

_____

_____

_____

3. How can you honor those around you who cannot honor
   you back?

_____

_____

_____

DAY 2

The Least of These

Commentary

In today's reading, Jesus spoke about his return at the end of the age and how he will separate people, as a shepherd separates the sheep from the goats. The goats were viewed negatively, while the sheep were viewed in a positive light. The criteria Jesus uses for this separation may seem surprising.

In Matthew 25:34, Jesus explained that when he returns, he will say to the righteous (the sheep), "Come . . . take your inheritance." Here's why: They fed him when he was hungry, invited him in when he was a stranger, clothed him when he was in need, cared for him when he was sick, and came to visit him in prison.

The righteous would ask him what he meant, and he would tell them that whatever they did to the least of his brothers and sisters, they did for him.

On the other hand, in Matthew 25:41–46, Jesus described how he would tell the unrighteous to depart from him. This is because they did not feed him when he was hungry, invite him in when he was a stranger, clothe him when he was in need, nor help him when he was sick and in prison. Jesus explained that the things they failed to do for the least of his brothers and sisters, they failed to do for him.

Jesus wants us to extend our kindness to those in need. If there's someone in your life who needs to be fed, clothed, and cared for, how can you show them kindness? It doesn't have to be a huge gesture. It can be as simple as buying gas for someone who is low on funds or bringing a home-cooked meal to a sick or grieving family member or neighbor. A part of our call as Christians is to serve others and give as though we are giving to Jesus himself.

Lord, thank You for reminding me how important it is to care for others. Please help me prioritize it more. Amen.

Discussion Questions

1. Is there anything you find challenging or inspirational about Jesus's words in today's reading?

   _____

   _____

   _____

2. As a woman, do you find it vulnerable or empowering to help others? Easy or difficult?

   _____

   _____

   _____

3. What are some practical ways in which you can serve someone in your community?

   _____

   _____

   _____

The Tax Collector's Repentance

Commentary

Zacchaeus was a wealthy tax collector who lived in the city of Jericho. Jesus happened to be passing by, and when Zacchaeus realized it, he climbed up a sycamore-fig tree so he could see him. Jesus noticed Zacchaeus and told him to come down. He practically invited himself over to Zacchaeus's house, and the tax collector welcomed him in.

People started to gossip as they saw what was happening. How could Jesus go to Zacchaeus's house? He was a tax collector, and therefore, one of the worst sinners. Tax collectors were Jewish people who were loyal to the Romans and overtaxed their brothers and sisters to make a profit for themselves.

Although Zacchaeus had a reputation for being a tax collector, he did something unexpected. He stood up and pledged to give away half of his possessions to the poor and pay back up to four times anything he had cheated out of others.

Responding to Zacchaeus's pledge, Jesus explained that salvation had come to his house. Zacchaeus was truly a son of Abraham (both physically and spiritually) because his heart was transformed by Jesus's Gospel.

Two important things signal Zacchaeus's change of heart. First, he welcomed Jesus gladly. Second, he decided to give abundantly to the poor and repay those he had stolen from. This teaches us that there is something about a heart transformed by the Gospel that leads someone to be welcoming of others and practice generosity.

Are you welcoming toward others? Your home doesn't have to be spotless to invite someone in. You don't have to be the perfect cook, either. A willingness to love others as Jesus loves you is all you need. Keep your arms wide open toward others in the same way that Jesus had his arms wide open toward you.

Lord, please show me how I can be more
welcoming toward others around me. Amen.

Discussion Questions

1. What does Jesus's interaction with Zacchaeus teach you about his heart toward all people?

_____

_____

_____

2. Can you think of a time when someone was particularly welcoming toward you? What happened?

_____

_____

_____

3. What are some things you have done to welcome others in your community?

_____

_____

_____

The Good Samaritan

Commentary

The Good Samaritan story is unique to the Gospel of Luke. In Luke 10:25, an expert in the law asked Jesus what he should do to inherit eternal life. Jesus responded with a question: "What is written in the law?" The expert explained that loving God and loving one's neighbors is written in the law. Wanting to feel good about himself, the expert asked, "Well, who is my neighbor?"

This is when Jesus told the parable of the Good Samaritan. A man was attacked by robbers on his way to Jericho. A priest passed by and ignored him. A Levite, another important Jewish leader, ignored him as well. Finally, a Samaritan man was passing by and helped him. Note that Samaritans and Jews didn't get along *at all*. (While today we use the term "Samaritan" to describe a helpful person, in biblical times, Samaritan referred to the people of Samaria.)

The Samaritan went above and beyond to be hospitable toward the injured man. He got him a hotel and told the hotel manager to care for him and give him whatever he needed. After telling the parable, Jesus asked the expert, "Which person was a neighbor to this man?" He responded correctly: "The one who had mercy."

It is easy to overlook someone in need. You may feel that you are not equipped to help or that someone else will come by and help. However, like the Good Samaritan, you can be a neighbor to those around you, wherever you are. Show mercy as Jesus does.

Is there someone in your life who could use your support? God wants you to reach out and help them. Do your best to show Jesus's love to this person. It may feel difficult or uncomfortable, but by helping, you may end up making a difference in their life.

Lord, help me be aware of the person in my life who is in need so I may support them when I can. Amen.

Discussion Questions

1. Why do you think the priest and the Levite ignored the injured man?

_____

_____

_____

2. Are there any character traits of the Good Samaritan you hope to emulate in your life?

_____

_____

_____

3. How do you personally fulfill Jesus's requirement to love your neighbor?

_____

_____

_____

Welcoming All

Commentary

Matthew 10:40–42 is a short reading filled with a lot of truth. First, in verse 40, Jesus taught his disciples that when others welcomed them, they were truly welcoming Jesus. Similarly, those who welcomed Jesus welcomed the Father who sent him. Think about how it would feel for you if someone willingly welcomed your child into their community. Wouldn't it feel as though they were welcoming you?

Next, he explained that those who welcome a prophet will receive a prophet's reward. A prophet was someone who spoke God's Word. By receiving a prophet, they would be helping the prophet's ministry and playing a part in their work. Jesus also explained that those who welcome a righteous person would receive a righteous person's reward.

Finally, in verse 42, Jesus said that the person who gives a cup of water to a little one who is his disciple will be rewarded. Although "little one" could be referring to a child, it more likely speaks of someone who is considered "little" in the realm of social standing and is overlooked by more prominent members of their community.

These verses explain that Jesus values when we welcome those who are his followers and do his will. We may naturally gravitate toward welcoming someone who is a prophet—or in today's world, a preacher or missionary. Perhaps you welcome fellow followers of Jesus with open arms. This is a rewarding thing to do. However, he desires that we welcome even the disciple who may be overlooked by others. As mentioned on page 160, welcoming even the "least" of Jesus's followers is like welcoming Jesus himself. God is pleased when, out of the kindness of your heart, you welcome those who he loves.

Lord, may I always have a heart to welcome those who You love, regardless of whether they are prominent or overlooked members of society. Amen.

Discussion Questions

1. Does anything surprise or impress you about Jesus's words in this passage? If so, what?

\
\
\

2. If there are rewards for welcoming Jesus's disciples, what do you think they might be?

\
\
\

3. How does it feel when others welcome you? What are some things you can do to help keep your heart open toward others?

\
\
\

Reflect and Take Action

Weekly Reflection

- Christian hospitality looks like inviting and welcoming people in who would otherwise not be welcomed.

- A part of our Christian calling includes serving others and giving to them as though we are giving to Jesus himself.

- Your home does not have to be perfect or spotless for you to be hospitable toward a neighbor. You only need a willingness to love others as Jesus loves you.

- Even when it is more convenient to ignore someone else's needs, God wants us to do the right thing by reaching out and helping.

- Ask Jesus for the heart to welcome his disciples, both the ones who are prominent and those who are overlooked in society.

Activity of the Week

This week we discussed the importance of Christian hospitality. It is an important practice for followers of Jesus. Hospitality does not come easily to everyone, and that's okay. For this activity, we will practice. Choose someone you don't usually talk to or spend time with. You may want to invite them into your home and have a conversation over dinner, or perhaps you can suggest that they join you for an afternoon walk. Whatever you choose, be willing to step out of your comfort zone to share Jesus's love with a brother or sister in Christ.

A Final Note

Hopefully this book has been an encouraging resource for you in your journey to strengthen your Christian faith. We covered a lot, but God's Kingdom is vast and so is the Bible. This is just the beginning. There is so much to learn, and as you discover Christ's teachings, your faith will flourish and grow deeper. As a woman created by God, you have so many wonderful gifts within you. Perhaps empathy, compassion, and the ability to express your feelings may be among your strengths. Maybe you enjoy teaching others and leading them to truth. Perhaps you love being with children, or maybe you're empowered by the presence of other adults. Seek out God's wisdom and allow him to cultivate your gifts. Surround yourself with others in faith who can lift you up, and be sure to look out for those around you who can use some support in their journey. And always remember, God loves you!

Group Study Guide

1. Go around the room and share a word or phrase that stood out to you from today's reading. What do you notice about this word/phrase?

2. What do you believe is the context surrounding this passage?

3. Is there a character in this passage you identify with most? Why?

4. What does this passage teach you about God's character?

5. What new insight have you learned about yourself or others after reading this passage?

6. Does this passage teach you anything about the world in general?

7. Are you currently wrestling with anything within this passage? If so, what?

8. Besides the lesson in today's reading, what is one way you can apply this passage in your life?

9. How do Jesus's teachings in this passage impact your relationships with friends and family?

10. What is one thing you plan to do differently in your life based on this week's reading?

11. Does being a woman change the way you would respond to the lesson in this reading?

12. What is your takeaway from this week's discussion?

Scripture Index

Acknowledgments

I would not have been able to write this book without the support and kindness of my husband, David; my parents; and my family and friends who have wholeheartedly believed in me and my words. I would also like to thank the Callisto team for the opportunity to write this book.

About the Author

 **SHANTÉ GROSSETT O'NEAL** is the founder of Daily She Pursues, an online ministry where she helps Christian women pursue a deep and lasting relationship with God. Alongside her ministry, Shanté is pursuing a master's degree in Biblical Studies at Liberty University. In her free time, she enjoys journaling, visiting museums, and reading good books. Find out more at dailyshepursues.com.